ISAAC'S WAY HOME

A MOTHER'S MEMOIR

Laura Hershberger

ISBN 978-1-64468-459-7 (Paperback)
ISBN 978-1-64468-460-3 (Digital)

Covenant Books, Inc.
11661 Hwy 707
Murrells Inlet, SC 29576
www.covenantbooks.com

This book is dedicated to our friends at
Edmarc Hospice for Children
In Portsmouth, Virginia.
They walked alongside us
and provided hope for the journey
from the very beginning.
Their unconditional support, encouragement,
and love for our family inspired me to share our story,
in hopes that it may provide greater awareness for
perinatal hospice and the other services they offer
to the greater Hampton Roads area.
After all, Virginia is for Lovers.

Introduction

Who knows if you have not become queen for such a time as this?
—Esther 4:14

The week before Christmas, I found myself reflecting on my life growing up, in order to apply for the next stage of my life in graduate school. With only a year of adulting under my belt after finishing my undergraduate degree in physical education, I did not feel very qualified to talk about overcoming challenges. Yet there I was, writing about why I wanted to become a social worker and the things that I wanted to see change in the world. At twenty-two, it was almost laughable how bright eyed and bushy tailed I was.

My personal essay consisted of three major points: helping children in the foster system, working with juvenile justice students, and being an advocate for families raising special-needs kids. I was embarrassingly naive to the level of need there was in this field, but the fact remains that this is still my core passion to this day. The heartbreak I have seen as a counselor for at-risk youth these last fifteen years ultimately taught me about resiliency. If I had not borne witness to all these incredibly resilient students and families, I may not have been able to find my own foundation in hope when I needed it most.

In truth, as I began to put pen to paper for this memoir, I found myself rereading many old blog posts I had written and emails I had sent to gain a little perspective. I could see the instances of my life that were preparing me for my hardest battle to date. It is very rare to find a lesson in hard circumstances while you are in the midst of them. Sometimes, the anger, the fear, the loss, and the hurt overwhelm me on anniversaries of those difficult times. Ultimately though, when I have enough distance from an event to allow me time to process and reflect, it gives me a second chance to see how my own strength and my community of supporters got me through to the other side.

Chapter 1

And we know that in all things God works for the good of those who love him, who have been called according to his purpose.
—Romans 8:28

My youngest child started preschool this past fall. On welcome day, a parent packet was sent home with information about the school year and what to expect those first few days. My daughter was given a scrapbook page to decorate with things about her and our family. We brainstormed about what she wanted her classmates to know about her and took a trip to the craft store to choose special stickers to decorate with. My daughter predictably picked out a pack of unicorn stickers. As we placed our most recent family photo from our summer sunflower session onto the middle of the purple cardstock paper, I asked my daughter what she wanted to be when she grew up. She answered immediately and without hesitation that she wanted to be a mermaid. Yes, I thought, this is definitely my child. While at her age, I was likely dreaming of being an Olympic swimmer. Her answer reminded me of my earliest memories of the job that I wanted to have when I grew up.

Gold medal winning aside, my biggest hope for my life has always been to be a mom. As an only child of a stay-at-home mother, I had a live-in role model while I was growing up. She was a Pinterest mom before that was a thing, doing crafts with me after school. She sang in the church choir, sat for hours timing at my swim meets, and was there to pick me up from school every day that I can remember. Everyone said I was her twin in looks and personality, and that was a compliment I hoped to live up to. She was my biggest fan, my best friend, and the one who saw things in me that ultimately led me on my future career path. My dad was right there alongside her every step of the way, cheering me on. Every night when I was little, he read to me at bedtime. As I grew older, he helped me with the hard parts of math, the edits on my English papers, and practicing my free-throw shot in the driveway. I definitely owe my love of reading and writing, in large part, to all of his support.

When it came time to apply for college, I decided on a tiny out-of-state private school that had the feel of an Ivy League campus but the same population of my small-town high school. I went practical with my education, declaring physical education and English as my major/minor degree, in hopes of following in my favorite junior high teacher, Miss Callis's footsteps. As luck would have it, I was on track to graduate early, so my mom, a college career counselor by then, recommended that I pick up a minor in sociology. After taking my first intro class, I was hooked. I found myself eagerly reading the book list and mapping out homework assignments days in advance. I loved everything about learning family dynamics and how our lives are affected by micro, meso, and macro levels of influence. It made sense to me, and I felt like I was seeing the world with new eyes. It didn't hurt that my professors saw this fire in me and told me I was a great candidate for pursuing an advanced degree in the field. This encouragement opened up a new path for me to move back to California and get my master's degree in social work with a school counseling credential. I combined my passion for sports and sociology into a 140-page thesis on a community assessment of adaptive aquatic programs for children with physical disabilities. I dedicated my first published work to my parents for all their support and editing along the way.

Once I finished school, it seemed like another box had been checked off of my proverbial type A to-do list. It was no surprise that I met and married my husband, Andrew, within the next year. We began the first chapter of our marriage, with him leaving for boot camp in Chicago for his six-year US Navy contract. After a long and cold year in the Great Lakes, we spent a quick sunny six months in San Diego to finish his schooling before getting his sea duty orders to Virginia. We were nervous to move all the way across the country from our families. The uncertainty of when Andrew would deploy and for how long made the thought of being three thousand miles away from my parents feel like a crazy plan. As much as I love to travel and feel brave about exploring new places, the thought that I would potentially be on my own for his nine-month deployment was daunting. In the end, I was more excited to put down some relatively long roots in the military with a four-year commitment to being on the East Coast. It didn't take long for us to get settled in and find our community in the area of Hampton Roads, Virginia. Little did we know just how serendipitous this place, and the people we met in it, would be to the events that unfolded.

Chapter 2

"For I know the plans I have for you," declares the Lord, "plans to prosper you and not to harm you, plans to give you hope and a future."
—Jeremiah 29:11

Upon our arrival in Norfolk, Virginia, I was eager to get plugged in as we prepared for my husband Andrew's anticipated deployment. We were renting a small house close to his job at Little Creek Naval Base and hoping to find a church close to the area. I googled non-denominational churches in a ten-mile radius from us, and the first thing that popped up was called Harvest Church Central. Barely a day after our moving truck's arrival, we attended our first Sunday morning service. I will never forget that it was the first weekend in October because they had their monthly newcomers' coffee that Sunday night. We broke out of our comfort zone and came back that evening to meet the staff. By the end of the night, I had introduced myself to the children's ministry director, in hopes that volunteering in the nursery might be a good way to meet other people while Andrew was away. That Wednesday also happened to be the kick-off for their fall small groups, and we found it appropriate that their slogan was "Don't do life alone."

We became fast friends with a group of about six other young married couples, many of whom were also in the military. It was nice to be with a group of people who were at a similar stage in life as we were: under thirty, married less than five years, thinking about starting a family and, most of all, being military transplants to the area. By the time Andrew got orders to deploy on Veteran's Day weekend,

I knew that I was in good hands with that core group of military wives from our new Bible study and church.

The night before Andrew left, I made him a going-away early Thanksgiving dinner. We knew that time apart would be hard, but the thought of going through all the major holidays during this first deployment was extra difficult. The morning Andrew left, I drove him to Norfolk International Airport. I parked the car, and we walked in together, dreading the moment we had to say goodbye. It was like those military commercials you see during Christmas, where the wife is silently crying as she watches her husband's camo bag go around the corner into the ticketed-passenger-only security line. I hadn't expected to be so emotional. But suddenly, I felt the enormity of sending the other half of my heart halfway around the world. It seemed like such an out-of-body experience to be a Navy wife at that time as the reality of Andrew's flying into the Middle East sat heavy on my mind.

As I drove around the airport loop, the beauty of the fall leaves and the smell of the first snow were just around the corner. This unfamiliar place was taunting me as I turned on my GPS to navigate my way back to a place that didn't quite feel like home yet. I forgot all of the things I had told myself leading up to Andrew's deployment about how awesome this new place was going to be. In truth, I had never felt so alone. I barely ate that night as I sat in our empty house, curled up with a blanket on the new couch we had purchased the month before. I absentmindedly turned on the TV and sat staring at but not seeing the menu guide. Was this going to be my life for the next few months? My thoughts began to swirl, allowing every negative thing I had worried about to come racing loudly to the forefront of my mind. Would I be able to find a job? Was our neighborhood really that safe? Would I ever make friends who would be in my contact list labeled as someone I could call if I needed to talk after a rough day?

In my state of anxiety, my heart began to hurt. Not like the heartbroken hurt that I felt deep in my soul from saying goodbye to Andrew but the kind of hurt that felt like I was having a heart attack. I had only felt that kind of hurt once, about three years before. At that time, the feelings of not having control over my own life came on the day my master's thesis was returned. I hadn't edited my page numbers correctly, so I was facing reformatting 140 pages with the deadline ticking. Back then, I didn't know what was going on.

I've struggled with anxiety since junior high. Initially, it looked a lot like I had a very strong type A personality. From the outside looking in, my perfectionism was apparent as I strove not just to be involved in everything but good at everything. I was a dual-sport athlete, with swimming added on to whatever seasonal thing I was doing at the time. I was actively involved in my church choir and school band. By fifteen and a half, I took my summer lifeguard job and turned it into a year-round coaching position with the local swim team.

I was the kid in college who never left a paper until the last minute and always did the extra-credit assignment. I was so hard on myself that when I got my first ever C grade on a psychology paper, it totally squashed my budding interest in counseling. When I graduated from an out-of-state private school after four years and moved home, I felt like I was going backward. I have always been future driven, focusing on the next phase of life to be accomplished.

When I waited till the last week before my grad school application was due to have my entrance essay edited by my dad, I knew I wasn't ready. I took a gap year to work at a residential group home in Sacramento for kids with mental health and behavior problems in the foster system. I figured if I could survive in these so-called social work "trenches," I could do anything. Two years later, I had to have my mom drive the forty-five minutes out to campus to pick me up during my first full-blown panic attack.

When I was in grad school, my doctor refused to give me anti-anxiety medication and told me it was just a tough season in life. His thought was that as soon as I walked across the stage and got my master's diploma in hand, I would be a happy camper and ready to enter the work world full time. Instead, that old nagging drive to be at the top of my field had me simultaneously going back to school for my school counseling credential, working full time at a non-profit, coaching swimming for three overlapping seasons, and pursuing my licensed clinical social work (LCSW) certification.

I was easily putting in eighty hours a week, with no social life in sight. When we were assigned to do a self-care project for homework in one of my night classes, I laughed and thought that no social worker in the history of time had ever thought about taking care of himself or herself first, and that was so true for me. Everything and everyone came before me, and I was exhausted.

When I graduated the next year, I married my husband just four short months after being reintroduced. It was like I had finally slowed down enough to see what I needed and found this incredible man to come along and support me in my crazy career.

Now that man I counted on as my rock was on a plane to meet up with his ship in Bahrain, and I felt completely overwhelmed by not having a plan for myself while he was away. I drove the half mile to the nearest hospital. I sat hyperventilating on the cold concrete waiting room floor until they had space to take me back. I spent six hours in the emergency room as the staff did the standard EKG test that I have become so used to when my anxiety gets out of control.

This time, the Navy doctors knew better than to tell me this was just a season or a phase, and they started me on a low dose of anti-anxiety medication and referred me to a counselor. I have learned that my mind's spiraling thoughts light up my nervous system and seep out in physical pain as my body tries its best to cry for help. This cry for help turned into an opportunity for friendship. The doctors wouldn't discharge me without having someone waiting to pick me up. They wouldn't even let me call a taxi. It needed to be a friend. I had two phone numbers from the Bible study group in my contact list, Sara and Ashley. I called the one who lived closest to me. Sara showed up in less than ten minutes to take me home. That night, we agreed that we would form a deployment wife group with Ashley. We celebrated Thanksgiving together at Ashley's house. Sara and I laughed our way through Zumba workout videos and had weekly dinners at my place. I even helped out in Ashley's classroom after many late nights of her doing school prep in my living room. My support system was growing.

During the four months Andrew was out to sea for the tail end of his ship's deployment, I took over as children's ministry director at Harvest (which later ended up renaming itself Upward Church). My connections continued to grow as I networked within the church. When Andrew came home Super Bowl weekend in February, I felt more at home in Virginia than I had anywhere else. I drove the quick ten minutes over to base and sat at the check-in gate behind a long line of cars all heading to the port to welcome the fleet home. I didn't know the families of any of Andrew's shipmates since he had flown out mid-deployment. I stood outside the pier, bundled up in my favorite khaki J.Crew peacoat, watching and waiting for the Whidbey Island amphibious ship to dock. I looked around at all of the people with welcome home signs, flowers, balloons, and new babies waiting to greet their loved ones. It clicked that this was truly an amazing community to be a part of, something bigger than oneself. I also realized the importance of having a supportive village standing behind me, to fill in the holes of the challenges being a military wife can otherwise have.

As the ship pulled in, I scanned the top deck for Andrew. It didn't take me long to find him standing tall and proud among the hundreds lining the edge of the ship. I would recognize the man's stance anywhere, even with everyone matching in their navy-blue dress uniforms. I smiled watching all the new fathers greeting their babies for the first time as they were the group of sailors given priority coming off the ship. I wondered impatiently how long it would finally be before Andrew got off. When I saw him, I waved through the chain-link fence and ran the length of the parking lot to where they were coming out of the gate. This sweet reunion was even better than when we had celebrated his boot camp graduation two years prior. I was so thankful to have my husband home on safe ground and back for the foreseeable future.

After every deployment, the big ships stay in port on shore rotation. Theoretically, this allows for them to do the annual maintenance needed and gives families time together. We were told we could anticipate having eighteen months that the ship would, at the very most, only be traveling stateside along the East Coast. We decided that it was as good a time as any to start a family. We celebrated the initial two weeks of Andrew's military leave with a vacation down south to the Outer Banks in North Carolina.

During our trip, it felt so normal to be back together, on a new adventure exploring the coast and going lighthouse hunting. We talked about our dreams of having a baby and wondered how being parents would work with Andrew's Navy career. Even though he was home, he still had overnight-duty days at least once a week. And the schedule for stateside deployments could have him gone for weeks at a time. We weighed the reality of these absences against future ten- to twelve-month deployments and knew that we needed to take advantage of this timeline.

The only hitch in our plan was my uncertainty about being able to have kids. As much as I had always longed to be a mother, and with the last years of my twenties winding down, I was nervous that my long-standing diagnosis of endometriosis would crop up and wreak havoc. When I was eighteen and just a semester into my first year at Whitworth College in Spokane, Washington, I ended up in the emergency room with severe abdominal pain. The doctors thought that I needed to have my appendix out. They called my parents in California and told them they may need to hop on a plane. I had a few more tests run, including an ultrasound, and it was determined that my appendix had not burst, but rather, I had a very large ruptured cyst. The ER doctors discharged me with a referral to the local specialty ob-gyn where I was diagnosed as having endometriosis.

It felt like such a potentially life-changing thing when I started researching about my diagnosis when I was in college. I had a family history of pregnancy challenges and wondered how this news would affect my chances to have a baby. On my way back from the doctor's office, I parked my car outside of my dorm and walked across the snowy campus quad to my best friend Julia's room. We sat at the very end of the hallway outside of her door, and I cried on her shoulder about the loss I felt of not knowing if a family was in the cards for me after all.

Later that week, I started my first internship at the local crisis nursery center and let silent tears fall as I held a six-week-old baby who had been born addicted to cocaine. A new purpose started to creep into my thoughts about providing a safe place for babies in foster care. I was only a freshman in college, but I started to dream about what it would be like to be an emergency foster mom for babies. My hope for a family turned into giving that hope to those whom it had been taken away from.

Fast-forward ten years to when I was reintroduced to Andrew. It was my birthday weekend, and I was out to dinner with some friends. A guy came out onto the back patio where we were sitting, and I nudged my friend and asked if she remembered him. Sure enough, we realized we had all gone to church youth group together in junior high and high school. He was a year younger than us though, and neither of us had known him well then. I smiled politely at him as we left the restaurant and wondered why I had never run into him before in our small town. The next morning at church, I came out of the service to meet up with a friend who was taking me out for my birthday lunch. Lo and behold, the same guy from the patio the night before, Andrew, stood there talking to my lunch date. I laughed shyly, and we reintroduced ourselves.

It turned out that I had been in a Bible study with his parents for the past couple of months without realizing that he also had moved home. I boldly suggested he should come with them some time. Later that night, we found each other on Facebook and stayed up chatting on messenger. Before I signed off, Andrew asked me out on our first date. I knew the first week we hung out that I wanted to marry him. He was the kindest, most humble person I had ever met, and the fact that we came from such similar upbringings made imagining a future family with him something I knew I wanted to pursue. We were married just four months later.

He left for boot camp just six weeks after our wedding, and it wasn't until our six-month anniversary that we actually got to move in together in the naval-base housing in Chicago. With the uncertainty of how long Andrew would be in school and when he would get orders for sea duty, our family plans were on hold. That is, until we drove cross-country from San Diego to Virginia and decided it was time, two years later. Unfortunately, with no positive pregnancy test results after trying for six months, I had a feeling my endometriosis was to blame. My doctors back in California had said they wouldn't do any surgery until I was ready to start a family. I met the local Navy obstetrician, and they agreed it was time for the laparoscopy.

Four months later, on our third wedding anniversary that December, about ten minutes before Andrew would get home from work, I took a pregnancy test. I waited in our tiny bathroom, admiring its bold orange walls and antique crystal doorknobs, anything to pass the time before my three-minute alarm rang with my results. Andrew came home from work like any normal day, and I walked out of the bathroom and around the corner and met him in the living room. I silently held up the positive pregnancy test with the cheesiest grin on my face. In one giant step, he closed the distance between us and hugged me so tightly I could feel my shoulders melt with relief that we were going to have a baby. That weekend, we drove to Busch Gardens near Williamsburg to celebrate our anniversary and our baby news. It was blissfully magical under the sparkling twinkle lights of Christmas Town.

Chapter 3

For a long time, there were only your footprints &
laughter in our dreams & even from such small
things we could not wait to love you forever.
—Brian Andreas, StoryPeople

It felt like the longest three months of my life, carrying around the happy news that I was pregnant. I am a terrible secret-keeper when it comes to happy surprises. I have a tendency to find the perfect gift for a family member and then not be able to wait until the holiday to give the present. When Andrew and I tried to come up with creative ways to tell our parents I was pregnant, we thought it would be incredible to walk off of the plane on New Year's Day and nonchalantly have me open my coat to reveal a sign reading "baby on board." Instead, I broke the news to them by Skype a week earlier on Christmas Day. It was one of the best Christmas surprises to be able to share the news with our parents in California that we would soon be calling them grandma and grandpa. It was a wonder that I made it as long as I did without sharing the good news about the baby with our closest friends.

At the beginning of the new year, many of our Bible study friends were either new moms or expecting soon. Also, in the wider church women's group, there seemed to be a new baby announcement at every monthly Friday ladies' night out. So much so that we had a running joke of who would get pregnant next. As a military church community, it wasn't uncommon to have large batches of babies all born around the same time, a phenomenon frequently called "homecoming babies," referring to when the large Navy ships would come back from long deployments.

During our February women's group, I had signed up to carpool with two fellow Navy church wives to drive down to Virginia Beach. Having just met these ladies, we were chatting through the usual get-to-know-you questions when one of them started talking about kids. Merely two weeks shy of my three-month marker, I confided in them that I was expecting my first baby. Looking back, I cannot believe I shared this big secret with near strangers. Just months later, I would learn that Marisa, the driver of the carpool, was also expecting her first child. By the time my delivery date came, there were nineteen women altogether at our church of around five hundred members who had babies within six months of one another.

With my position in children's ministry being so visible, it was not long before everyone in the church knew of our happy news. When it came time to have our gender scan appointment, I had already put out a poll on Facebook to vote on whether we were going to have a boy or a girl. Our friends were 50/50 on guessing pink or blue. Andrew had taken the day off from work, and we went in first thing in the morning for my ultrasound. We arrived early at the naval base to make sure we could find a parking space in the only garage located next to the hospital. The radiology office was on the first floor, at the very end of the hallway. As I checked in at the front desk for my ultrasound, I felt like I was announcing my new pregnancy to the waiting room.

The nurse ushered us back to get my vitals done before taking Andrew and me into a small room for me to change into my hospital gown. The sonographer came in, and I could immediately tell she liked her job. She was cheerful and kind with her small talk as she turned off the lights and helped me lie back in the bed. The ocean scene panels on the ceiling reminded me of the cute decorations from a pediatric ward.

"Now this might feel a little bit cold," the technician warned me as she added jelly to the ultrasound wand and placed it just above my right hip bone. "I can tell you did a great job of hydrating this morning. It helps me to see the baby clearly."

I laughed as I looked at Andrew and joked, "It also makes me feel like I'm going to pee my pants a little bit." But I don't think he heard me because he was too distracted looking at the screen, where we were getting the first glimpse of our baby.

"Looks like you have a yoga baby in there," the technician said. "Those are the little legs up over the baby's head."

No wonder I could feel gymnastics going on in my stomach, I thought, smiling.

"And here you have the mouth and a sweet button nose." She continued to rattle off body parts as she went about labeling them on her screen and then clicked Print. "Have you decided if you want to know the sex of the baby?" she asked.

I shyly smiled at Andrew, and we nodded in agreement. "Yes, that would be great," I said. "Can you tell what it is from this position?"

The technician made an arrow symbol on the screen, typed the word "boy," and again clicked Print. As I watched another ultrasound image come out of the printer, I squeezed Andrew's hand, feeling the tears welling up in my eyes.

The tech handed us some of the ultrasound pictures that had curled up like a long receipt from the grocery store cashier. Andrew and I looked adoringly at the first pictures of our son.

"I'll give you guys a minute alone while I go grab the doctor," the tech said as she got up from behind the computer screen. "There are some measurements in the brain that I want him to take a look at before you leave." Our moment of celebration was short-lived as I looked at Andrew wide-eyed and wondered what the tech had seen that she had not shared with us.

I was ready for my bathroom break by the time the doctor came in, and my anxiousness to hear what the doctor had to say made me feel even more uncomfortable. The doctor introduced himself quickly and went right to the wand and began rolling it over my belly to find the best view of our son's head.

"Can you see this dark area here?" he asked us as he pointed to the screen and showed us what looked like the top of the forehead. I craned my neck as best I could from my position on the exam bed and nodded silently. "The black area signifies an excess of fluid buildup around the brain. These measurements show the four quadrants of the brain pooling into one another, when they should in fact be clearly separated. The condition is called hydrocephalus. Once you get dressed, the front desk will schedule you for an appointment on the seventh floor at the neonatal specialty clinic. They will do a high definition ultrasound for you to provide more answers."

Andrew and I sat there stunned as the doctor conveyed this information calmly, shook our hands, and sent us on our way with the best of luck.

The front desk clerk gave me my appointment card for Friday, and Andrew and I began the walk hand-in-hand back to the car. As we rode the elevator up to the top deck of the parking garage, I looked at him and said, "Well, it's not great news, but it sounds treatable. The doctor didn't make too much of a fuss about the level of concern."

As Andrew drove us home, I googled the term *hydrocephalus* and prefaced the outcome out loud. What I read did nothing to calm my fears about the simple fact that our baby's brain was not what it should be. I wondered how that would affect his life. Would he be able to play sports? Would he be able to speak? The possibilities that ran through my mind of what this swelling was doing to his brain were endless.

We pulled up to the curb of our little Cape Cod rental home, and my phone was already pinging. The world of social media was eagerly awaiting news on who had won the pink-or-blue guessing game we had polled the night before. I could not bear to post anything on Facebook, and when close friends started texting me, I was at a loss of what to share. Eventually, I could not ignore all the inquiring minds, and I shared a cute picture I had found in anticipation of our gender reveal, a chocolate Hershey's bar with the HE highlighted in blue. Then I got on the computer and sent out an email to our closest family members.

Andrew and I lay in bed that night, talking about boy names and throwing out a variety of suggestions for middle name ideas to go with our planned familial first name. We discussed many Bible names like John, Luke, Levi, Matthew, Malachi, and Elijah (Eli for short). Then there were some other relatives' names like Liam (short for William) on Andrew's side, or Finn (short for Finley) on my side of the family. With other more current names I liked, Andrew teased me saying they sounded straight from a soap opera like Lucas, Ethan, and Jackson. These were all tested out in combination with our top first name at the time, Micah. Nothing stuck.

It seemed like the natural thing to do to pick out a name after finding out that we were having a boy. But it also seemed like such a lower priority when we had this possible diagnosis, and then some, hanging over our heads. I remember sharing with my mom the next day that "little boy blue" had some challenges ahead of him. I stumbled through recapping the ultrasound results and tried to keep a hopeful voice as I explained what I thought we might expect to hear from our upcoming appointment. While I was worried that our baby wasn't 100 percent healthy, I told Andrew I would be okay to go on my own to our follow-up appointment so he wouldn't have to miss work.

Chapter 4

Do not be anxious about anything, but in every situation, by prayer and petition, with thanksgiving, present your requests to God. And the peace of God, which transcends all understanding will guard your hearts and your minds in Christ Jesus.

—Philippians 4:6–7

On Good Friday of Easter weekend, I went into the neonatal specialty clinic. I was preparing myself mentally for a long day of complicated medical jargon as I waited for the bridge to open on my way to the Naval Medical Center Portsmouth (NMCP). When I arrived, I was ushered in to sit down with the kind-hearted geneticist to talk about my family medical history. She stood up to introduce herself and shook my hand across a small table in her cozy office. I pulled a chair to the tiny table that just barely fit in the middle of her room as she expertly swiveled her chair out from her corner desk and pulled up across from me. She drew out a diagram upside down so that I could read it normally from where I sat. I wondered how many times she had to have had this conversation with families to get so good at writing this chart, almost as if she could do it with her eyes closed. She rattled off some potential complications like cerebral palsy, spina bifida, and a few others that I had heard of. I told her that I was a social worker and had worked with many special-needs kids in previous jobs. I mentioned that I was so passionate about this particular at-risk population that I had written my master's thesis on an adaptive aquatic program for children with physical disabilities. Looking back now, I was bravely trying to remind myself that I had experience working with special-needs children and that it was nothing to be afraid of as a parent. I remember leaving her office to get my high-definition ultrasound and feeling confident that whatever they told me next, I could handle it with grace and poise.

The ultrasound felt very similar to the one I had had just days previously, with the technician commenting on what a beautiful and strong baby boy I had growing inside me. She took all the measurements and pictures and talked me through everything leading up to the brain. At this point, she became much quieter as she finished and let me know that the doctor would need to come in to look at the images herself. The neonatologist introduced herself and silently ran the wand over my belly, looking at the head from all different aspects. When she was done, I cleaned up and came back out to talk with her about what she had seen. Sitting there on the exam bed, I listened unbelieving as the doctor told me my son's brain was herniating out of the back of his skull. She continued in the most straightforward and flat tone that it was a condition called ventriculomegaly, with extreme hydrocephalus caused by an occipital encephalocele. I asked her for a pen, and I took out my purple pregnancy journal that the Navy hands out at your first gynecology appointment. I opened it to the notes page and asked her to repeat the diagnosis slowly so I could write it down. I knew I wouldn't remember all of this later.

"In normal healthy pregnancies," she started to explain, "around week five, the neural tube forms by the time most women even know they are expecting." In her best laymen's terms, she went on to explain, "But in these cases, the neural tube never completely formed."

I stared at her blankly, trying desperately to remember the chapters on conception from my college anatomy and physiology class.

Noting my confused look, she continued, "Essentially, it leaves a gap in the skull for cerebral spinal fluid to pool and push unformed parts of the brain outside of the head."

She paused for me to take it all in, but all I could ask was "What does that mean for my baby?"

She sat down on her doctor's stool, looked me straight in the eyes, and said, "It means you have five weeks to decide if you want to abort the baby as he is likely not going to live to term."

I started to cry, and she excused herself to let me have some time to process. Even in my devastation, I thought how cruel it was to leave a five-months-pregnant woman alone with her raw emotions to deal with the death sentence the doctor had just given my unborn baby.

I don't know how long I sat there and sobbed before she came back in and told me the geneticist would follow up with me for further information. As I walked back into the cozy office I had left less than an hour previously, I was truly in shock, thinking about all the common diagnoses I had prepared myself for. I never, for a second, imagined that our baby would not be compatible with life if he was born. It was clear at this point that the geneticist was the landing pad for my sorrows as she sat with me in my devastation. She explained that I had some options for follow-up testing to check for other types of disability indicators as well as genetic factors to determine if this was specific to my current pregnancy or if it would be a concern for any future children as well. I scheduled the necessary appointments at the secretary's desk and then proceeded to take the loneliest walk of my life through the large hospital and across the parking garage to my car. I thought of Andrew, who was at a work training. He had texted me, anxious to hear more about what the doctors had said. All I could muster in my short response was that it wasn't good and that I would explain when he got home.

Later that afternoon, I met Andrew on the front lawn of our perfect little Cape Cod rental house with the white picket fence and collapsed in his arms. The pain was unimaginable, having to explain to him what the doctors had told me earlier that day. We held onto each other, crying in a space of time that seemed to stand still around us. I couldn't bear the thought of telling anyone else about the details of our life-shattering news, but I knew our families would be wondering about the results. That evening, I stared at my blank email formatted to our parents and siblings. Words that normally flowed so easily across the distance from where we were in Virginia all the way to our loved ones in California would not come. I typed and deleted draft after draft, and when I finally hit Send, I felt as though I had just broken the hearts of everyone on my list.

Dear Family,

We are sad to share that today's doctor appointment did not go well. Baby boy's brain is hemorrhaging out of the back of his skull, which never fully developed. The prognosis is likely a miscarriage or stillbirth. I will be going in next week for a fetal echo, MRI, and an amniocentesis to see if any of this was specific to this pregnancy or if it will affect future babies. We appreciate your concern at this time but will likely not be up for talking on the phone over the next week as we try to make sense of this all. I have taken a week of personal leave from work for the time being, and Andrew is looking into how much the Navy will give him as well. Thank you for your prayers.

Love,
Andrew and Laura

I could hear the pain in their responses as I opened emails of prayer and sorrow from the would-be grandparents. This was the first grandbaby on both sides of the family. The loss was felt heavily on the West Coast that night. In particular, I thought of my mom reading our news. She had never pressured me to start a family, but we had talked many times of her dream of being a Nana. I also think the closeness of all the women in our family to their mothers is a particularly special relationship trait passed down between the generations. My mom was excited for me to live my dream of having a baby.

If I thought writing the words down in print would solidify the reality of our baby's diagnosis, it was nothing in comparison to imagining having to tell people face-to-face. Our church had multiple Easter services planned for the weekend, and Andrew and I decided we couldn't face all our friends just yet at our usual Sunday time. We ended up attending the Saturday night service, where I hoped we would come across fewer people looking to hear about the details of our gender reveal. At that point, people outside of our family were still completely unaware that there were any problems. When I walked in the front doors of our church and ran into one of my close Bible study friends and fellow pregnant mama Shannon, I immediately started to cry. She had congratulated me on our baby boy, and all I could do was to shake my head with my lips quivering. She scooped me up in a mom-to-mom hug, and I remember sobbing to her that the baby was not expected to make it out alive. I cried the rest of the night as we made our way into our usual seats at the aisle on the front right of the stage. My sensitive pregnancy nose wasn't even bothered by the heavily cologned man sitting a few rows behind us. I could barely keep my cries contained as our campus pastor's mother put her hand on my shoulder and asked if I was all right.

I can't recall who else I saw that night or what other people in our church we shared our sorrow with after the service, but that sermon has long been etched on my heart. That weekend, our pastor, Craig Walker, debuted a new series based off of his book, *The Last Minute God*. It became clear that Andrew and I were meant to be in that space, hearing those words that evening. The message touched on all the repetition of waiting that is written in the Bible. There were stories about pain and suffering, confusion and anger at life's circumstances that so many characters had witnessed or endured themselves. In each of these people's lowest valleys, there came an incredible rescue through healing or promise, goodness and miracles. Oftentimes, it was when their trust seemed to be wavering as they questioned their faith. Yet time and time again, God showed up, and He even showed off, proving that perseverance was rewarded with miracles only He could grant. When I left that night, all I could think about was the often-quoted phrase in church at Easter, "It's Friday, but Sunday's coming."

I clung to this sentiment and seemingly ironic timing in my own life. In Christian circles, this quote is a reference to Jesus dying on the cross for our sins on a Friday, only for His tomb to be found empty on Sunday and His followers to see that He had risen from the dead. I wondered if we would be so fortunate for a miracle. We heard of our baby's assumed fatal diagnosis that Friday but were holding onto the hope that somewhere in our future, we would be blessed with his life. This parallel brought such new meaning to my faith and the idea of God as a Father and the resurrection of His Son, Jesus. Somehow, through the depths of my despair, I knew that the only way that I would survive this unexpected journey of motherhood was to relinquish my selfish human control and give all my worries and anxiety over to God, a concept I had been reminded of weekly in our church's favorite slogan, "Don't do life alone."

Sometime that weekend, I went through my address book and forwarded my family email about our diagnosis results to our inner circle of friends. Andrew and I took the next few days off of work and walked around wondering what would happen next.

Chapter 5

We glory in our sufferings, because we know that suffering produces perseverance; perseverance, character; and character, hope.
—Romans 5:4

Just shy of a week after we got our baby's diagnosis, I went in for a full day of testing. Andrew and I spent eight hours in the hospital going to four different appointments that included a fetal echo, MRI, lab testing, and a much more in-depth meeting with the geneticist. I debated wearing my pajamas to the hospital that day but settled on my favorite pair of black pregnancy yoga pants and my most comfortable long-sleeve thermal. I had to fast for most of the testing, and I listened to my hungry baby belly yelling at me to eat breakfast as Andrew drove the all-too-familiar route past the Portsmouth harbor to the Navy hospital.

The fetal echo appointment was in the same clinic office as the ultrasound we had had when we first learned something wasn't right. I hated even sitting in the waiting room and remembering that terrible day. Thankfully, we quickly learned that our baby's heart was perfect. Our next stop at the MRI, however, got my anxiety swirling. At six months pregnant, I was strapped onto the gurney of the machine, covered in warm blankets, and given a pair of standard blue earplugs. I was frantic. I have a good amount of claustrophobia, and combined with my hatred of loud repetitive noises, I could not relax. I am sure it didn't help that my ever-present feeling of needing to pee made the forty-five-minute procedure a living nightmare. I couldn't get out of that place soon enough. With my belly still grumbling, we continued down the hall to the east wing to wait in line at the lab. I checked in at the front desk, where they gave me a nasty orange liquid to drink. It was a two-part series, but thankfully, I was finally allowed to eat in between.

We rode the elevator to the cafeteria and got a quick bite to eat at Subway. Then we grabbed the elevator again and went up to the maternity floor. This visit with our geneticist felt like an interview to work for the CIA. We were asked all sorts of crazy questions about family health history and had to keep a running tab of what to follow up with our parents when we didn't know the answer. I had done my Google research before the visit and knew that encephaloceles had no known cause. But this shakedown for what ailed various family members made me wonder if there was a genetic component that would follow all future pregnancies we might have.

I was referred to a new primary doctor who would take over my care going forward with monthly checkups. I was saddened to leave the obstetrician I had been working with. When I told her my news, she shared that she, too, was a Christian and that she would be praying over our family. In contrast to all the ways the cold neonatal specialty office had left me alone in my grief, this woman's care and concern filled the room as she made space for me to share all of my sadness. With the nature of military medical care, I never actually saw my next obstetrician specialist twice, one of the many flaws in the system of going through a high-risk pregnancy. The lack of continuity between appointments made it that much more traumatic to have to re-explain my history and our choice to keep the baby, a decision that many of the highest-ranked officers tried to talk me out of.

I had always been pro-life. I never realized I would ever be in a situation where that was tested, let alone questioned so heavily. After that long day of testing, I can still picture us driving home from the hospital. The silence in the car between Andrew and me was palpable, but I had to ask the question out loud for confirmation. "We're going to keep the baby, right?" We looked at each other at the stoplight as we waited for the backed-up bridge traffic. Yes, we agreed. We were going to see this pregnancy through.

That first weekend in April, we had our initial visitors come to console us with food for our stomachs and prayers for our hearts. Our friends Frances and Aaron were just weeks away from expecting their first child. I had my pending RSVP for Fran's baby shower stuck on my fridge with my favorite "Virginia is for lovers" magnet. As soon as they received our news by email, they promptly asked when they could bring us dinner. The heart of their friendship shone through so deeply as they were in the midst of celebrating their upcoming due date, and we were mourning ours. When they arrived, Fran and Aaron stood outlined in the door opposite as could be. Her tiny frame, standing at maybe 5'3," was all baby belly, holding her vegetarian pasta dish just past her bump. Aaron towered behind her and had to bend coming into our historic house. Both had the look of desperate sorrow on their faces as we welcomed them inside with their sympathetic hugs.

Sitting in our sunny living room with the first signs of spring coming to life outside, I couldn't help but feel the shift in the air. We had hosted Bible study with Frances and Aaron in this space almost as many times as we had had them over for football nights. Now the tone of the visit was somber. I began to share with these sweet friends about our hope that this pregnancy would serve as a living testimony of our faith. The words began to tumble out, and the more I spoke, the stronger my resolve was to see this baby to term. I was so thankful for people who would sit and listen with affirming nods as I processed out loud for what felt like the first time. Later that night, as Andrew and I lay in bed, I found a little voice in the back of my head urging me to find a name for our baby. It felt like if we could honor our unborn child with a name, we would validate his life and confirm our confidence that we would get to meet him. One of my favorite things about names was the meaning behind them and the purpose and potential a name laid out for a child's life.

Initially, when we had talked about baby names, we had considered a familial male name on Andrew's side of the family. It was a sort of father/son tradition that he and his dad shared. We had always thought we would continue it should we have a boy of our own. That little voice was growing louder, and with its determination to name our son, another parallel Bible story came to the forefront of our conversation, one about a woman named Sarah whom I had long felt connected to.

This story tells of a husband and wife, Abraham and Sarah, who were not able to have children. When I was struggling with my endometriosis diagnosis in my twenties, I often thought of Sarah and how she waited for a child for many years. The story goes on to say that God told Abraham that he would not only be blessed with a son but that he would be the father of many nations. When Abraham told Sarah, they laughed at the thought of having their first baby when he was approaching the age of one hundred. Eventually, Sarah gave birth to a boy, and they named him Isaac, which means laughter.

As Isaac grows up, Abraham is called to the mountains to give a sacrifice to God. It becomes clear that it is not an animal that he must present but that God has asked Abraham to sacrifice his one and only son, Isaac. There is no explanation. Just this request. As Abraham and Isaac continue their journey, Isaac realizes that *he* is the sacrifice when his father begins to bind him. When father and son go through the motions of preparing the sacrifice, God comes in at the last minute and spares Isaac. Abraham is blessed for his faith in God's plan, and a ram is sacrificed instead.

Of course, I don't presume to say that we were called to sacrifice our son in this same way, but I related so much to the notion of offering our child to his heavenly Father. So we decided to name our son Isaac. Giving life to this name allowed us to bring voice to our prayers for our son and for all our wide network of prayer warriors who were beginning to come alongside us in our journey. From there, I knew it was time to open my heart in a way that would allow others to witness the testimony of our pregnancy, whatever the outcome might be. I started a blog called Hope4Isaac. In the months that followed, we reached more than 50,000 people across the United States, and many overseas, as friends and family shared our story in their own circles. This village of support was so evident as people from all over reached out to us with their love, encouragement, and prayers.

People from Andrew's work sent baked goods home with him. The Navy chaplain invited us over to his house for dinner. Our church family set us up on a meal train, and I barely even had to go grocery shopping over the next few months. I got comments on my church staff web page from people at our sister sites in Florida saying their congregation was praying for our family. We started to receive an exceptional amount of mail from people we had never met, who had heard our story shared by our friends or through social media. Without fail, our church body prayed over our family every Wednesday night. It was surreal to see how our story was linking us together to such a wide community.

I blogged honestly about my fears about the pregnancy and acknowledged when there were little celebrations to be had. I tried to explain complicated medical details to spare people from seeing the stomach-turning photos that might pop up alongside of the googled diagnosis. Mostly, I used the space of the internet to journal the good and the bad days and try to reflect when things, like my first Mother's Day weekend, arrived.

A Mother's Love
May 12, 2013

I recognized that I was born to be a mother before I got into junior high. I knew that God's biggest purpose for my life was to take care of His littlest children, whether they be my own or not. Along the way, this became more and more apparent with each babysitting or nanny job, coaching, summer camp, counseling, etc. And I don't pretend for one minute that this wasn't inspired by my own mother, who was a stay-at-home mom for me growing up. It was her example that inspired me to want to be present for the children in my life, in whatever form that took. And it was this also that led me to want to take care of at-risk youth whose parents weren't there for them like mine were.

But it wasn't until this year that I started to gain a more insightful perspective of the power of a mother's love, the power of my mom's love for me. When you see someone who cares about you experience your grief and hurting through a situation, you realize that they are doubly impacted because of their care and concern for you as well as their unborn grandchild. Life-changing moments like these also allow a new level of honesty about people's own experience with motherhood. There are quite a few amazing women in my family who have gone through their own difficult times with getting pregnant or miscarriages and other scary health issues with their children.

These women have so selflessly shared their stories with me in the tough times and let me into their own heartache that they have burdened with regards to their children. These examples have had a profound impact on me and our family circumstances as I am reminded of just how many people before me have trusted in God for a miracle of healing, and/or have relied on Him during their time of hurt. I have been blown away by the compassion these women have shown me and how they each, in their own way, have come beside me through this beginning journey of motherhood to share their support and encouragement. I know that I learn, from each of them, something to add to my parenting toolbox or lessons of love and loss to take away with me. I can't begin to think of being prepared for Isaac's arrival and what that will look like in adjusting to life as a mother with a special-needs baby, but I know that we will not be alone and that each and every woman I know will be just a phone call away.

So thank you for all you have done and continue to do. Happy Mother's Day, Mammas.

We celebrated a small victory with this growing community when we shared that the results of my long day of testing all came back negative. In the big picture, none of this changed Isaac's diagnosis, but it did bring comfort that there were no other challenges that any future children of ours would face. It did, however, highlight a harsh reality that there was no real rhyme or reason to the health conditions he was facing. Thus, the deep dive into Google research began, and my determination to learn all I that I could, replaced whatever fear I still had left.

- God is so wonderful and so amazing. This news is so encouraging. We will continue to pray each day for your family and your precious son. Love you. (Mama Pitt)
- God is sooo good! We will keep praying for you three! If you need anything, please let us know! Hugs! Love ya! (a fellow Navy wife)
- We serve such a big God! Continuing to pray for the 3 of you and all of God's "hands" He is putting in your path. Xoxo! (Bethany)
- What a blessing to have a meeting with the doc that fills you with HOPE! We will continue to pray for sweet Isaac (Cousin from Nebraska)

Chapter 6

The will of God will not take us where the
grace of God cannot sustain us.

—Billy Graham

My six-month checkup brought about the shift in our medical team's thinking that we were keeping the baby and that they needed to get on board with our decision and provide us with local resources. The first step was to meet with the ob-gyn social worker. This, in itself, was comforting, knowing that I could talk openly with someone in my professional line of work and, hopefully, walk away with some tangible support options in the Hampton Roads area. She was a beautiful woman with tight black curls and the type of chic outfit that screamed professional. I envied her in a way as I looked around her office, albeit small; it was decorated with empowering quotes and perfectly organized leaflets. I couldn't help but picture myself in her shoes and wish that I was the licensed clinician comforting the devastated pregnant woman. We talked about our shared profession and my experience in the field, although not medical; we bonded over the challenges of providing resources to people in need. She shook her head apologetically as she handed me the single piece of paper that seemed painfully insufficient for my grief that was so heavy and overwhelming. It was a chart listing local agencies that provided a variety of things for people in our situation where a loss was expected. She pointed to the highlighted local children's hospice agency and explained that it was mere blocks from the Portsmouth Naval Hospital.

In true Laura fashion, I went home and researched each of the things on my list. It felt like I should laminate the lone paper for safekeeping, since it was the sole bit of practical resources I had at my fingertips. In my mind, it may as well have been the directions explaining how to build a piece of furniture from Ikea. It looked simple at first glance, but when I sat down to try to navigate the instructions, I felt hopelessly lost and wondered if everyone else struggled this much. I started my checklist by calling Edmarc Children's Hospice first, per the Navy social worker's recommendation, to set up an intake appointment with the agency social worker. I also went online and checked out the variety of support groups listed at the local hospitals and emailed the organizers about whether or not our story would fit in with the majority of other parents in attendance. Unfortunately, it seemed as though our diagnosis didn't fall in the main categories of common birth defects, and none of the options felt like what I needed.

Ultimately, I reached out to an online community called Sidelines, where parents could be matched with volunteer mentors who had gone through similar health journeys with their kids. My specific request was to be paired with someone who had received a fatal diagnosis in utero. I wanted the advice, wisdom, and understanding of a mother who had carried her baby to birth, despite all the anticipated complications that were expected at delivery. With little practical advice available to me about having a complicated pregnancy, I was determined to get guidance from someone who had traveled this uniquely twisted road before me. I felt that if I could even hear some hard truths, it might help to strengthen my heart in preparation for the challenges that would inevitably come. Or maybe someone could even give me some advice on how others had planned for the worst while simultaneously grieving the process.

On the home front, we relied heavily on the support of our closest friends from our Bible study and our campus pastor, Tommy, and his wife, Laura. In between appointments and results, we tried our best to get into a routine of survival. Ironically, I had just landed my dream promotion. In addition to working part time at my church, I had taken a job with a local social service agency where I served as a house arrest counselor. I had never worked with this population of at-risk kids before, but I had been promised a transfer into their clinical internship program after six months. It turned out that my counseling background came in useful in the world of juvenile justice, and the probation department created a grant to bring me on board with them full time. The week that we were given the dreadful news of Isaac's diagnosis should have been my first week in my new position at the courthouse. Instead, my first day there turned into my first experience of having to explain to new coworkers that yes, I was pregnant, but that it was complicated. They were incredibly gracious and let me start part-time as I acclimated to my days of learning their computer system and all the differences between working in a therapeutic role and in a world of police-minded probation officers. There wasn't much else for me to do at that point as I built referrals for my caseload.

By the first week of May, we had our next ultrasound with disappointing news. Secretly, I had hoped that I would go in and hear that the condition of the excess cerebral spinal fluid was decreasing or, at the very least, stable. Sadly, Isaac's brain continued to swell, and the chances of survival without severe disability became smaller and smaller. I had not resigned myself to believing that all hope was lost, but I recognized that I needed to be prepared for the worst. Growing up, I had babysat for a little boy who had been born with a severe disability. I knew him when he was about three, and even at that point, he was wheelchair bound. I helped to feed and bathe him, but in my young teenage eyes, never realized what his care routine would be like long-term for his family. Now I thought about him and wondered if my son would soon be living a similar life.

As I waited for a match with Sidelines and my appointment at Edmarc, I found a book called *Waiting with Gabriel* by Amy Kuebelbeck. Amy's story is about her pregnancy with a baby boy who had a fatal heart condition. In it, she shared familiar feelings about carrying a child to term so publicly while also carrying the burden of a fatal diagnosis. This was the hardest part for me to grasp. Ordinary life was happening all around me. I would go to the grocery store, and people would congratulate me on my pregnant belly and ask all sorts of seemingly inappropriate questions and go way past my personal boundaries. Not a day went by when I wasn't approached by someone new who didn't know our story. How could I explain what was going on to complete strangers in a way that felt manageable?

One evening, I drove the half-mile down the street to our local grocery store for a few late-night-craving fixes. When it was my turn at the checkout line, I realized I had left my wallet at home. I started to cry big sobbing tears and said I would have to come back with my credit card. The sweet middle-aged lady behind me stepped up and asked the cashier how much I owed. It was just shy of twenty-five dollars, and she handed the checker the necessary cash. I sputtered my thanks as she smiled and said, "Pregnancy brain, I know that one. I have five kids." This simple kind gesture made me cry even harder as I got in my car and thought, *If only she knew.*

It seemed like every time I left the house, someone had an opinion or a story or comment about my pregnancy. I hated how normal it was for people to talk to me about it when I felt so protective of my truth. I wasn't even sure how I could share with friends who had just found out that we were expecting but hadn't yet heard of the sad diagnosis. I had no idea how to handle either situation, and the weight of anxiety that I carried about each of these interactions kept me awake many nights.

Often, I would wake up in the middle of the night and think that I had just had the worst nightmare, only to gently rub my kicking belly and realize the difficult truth. I was never in denial of our diagnosis news, but the overwhelming weight of the reality was a shock that took a long time to shake off. I still don't know how Andrew managed to get up and go to work every morning. His ship did the best they could to support him, and they connected him with the Navy chaplain and gave him some resources about a military program called the Exceptional Family Member Program (EFMP). While Andrew distractedly went about his daily testing of machinery and followed the strict checks and balances list at work, I was getting certified to teach anger management to youth who were court ordered to attend the program. I was consumed with guilt about finally being in a job that would take me to the next point in my career as a licensed clinical social worker where I could become a true therapist. It seemed like such cruel timing to have been given an opportunity to get everything I ever wanted on the job front, while simultaneously taking away my dreams for family. There was no having my cake and eating it too. If Isaac was born alive, and if he had all of these anticipated health issues, I knew I wouldn't be able to be a working mom. I also knew that if I became a full-time stay-at-home mom, I would likely be setting myself back years with such a gap on my résumé. I wanted to eat a slice of that celebratory cake so badly.

When Andrew and I went in for our first appointment with Edmarc, we were told that even our participation in the program was a relatively new concept. It seems as though many people who experience pregnancy loss go through miscarriage or abortion and do not often carry their babies to term and put them in hospice at birth. Nevertheless, the staff was well-prepared to offer us whatever familial support we needed in the remaining months of my pregnancy and for however long we had with Isaac after birth. Their program introduced us to a network of professionals who were able to advocate for us, explain complicated medical jargon after hospital checkups, refer us to additional local resources, and support us with many other comfort cares. Finally, I felt like I had some tangible things to add to my emotional toolbox for this journey.

I looked through the big folder our new hospice social worker, Britney, had given us to take home and review. I tucked my single piece of paper from the Navy social worker behind all the new handouts. Now I had more than just websites and phone numbers to look up or call. I had times and dates of grief groups, details about local hospital parent support meetings and, most importantly, a calendar of events where I could meet the community of people who were all going through this child hospice thing together.

Chapter 7

Therefore I tell you, whatever you ask for in prayer, believe that you have received it, and it will be yours.
—Mark 11:24

Armed with a team of medical and emotional professionals on speed-dial, Andrew and I went to our first appointment with the neurosurgeon at NMCP. We quickly found out that there was no pediatric specialist on site; for us to choose this option, we would either be sent to Philadelphia Children's Hospital (CHOP) or to our local King's Daughters. Our Navy doctor was an extremely kind man but also very honest. He told us that he had never performed the specific surgery that Isaac would need because of the rarity of the diagnosis. He recommended we get a second opinion and decide where we wanted to have the surgery. I felt like I had just been given a hard dose of reality from a favorite uncle, knowing that he had our best interests in mind as he shared his opinion.

It wasn't a hard decision then, when we ended up meeting the top pediatric neurosurgeon at our local children's hospital. His blunt and curt manner regarding the chances of survival Isaac faced left no room for warmth or understanding. He sat behind his big mahogany desk, with a wall of windows behind him overlooking the hospital garden quad. His eyes scanned the images we had brought with us as he told us, in no uncertain terms, that he probably wouldn't take the case because he wouldn't waste his time operating. I left the appointment in tears, thinking we had just witnessed the stereotypical brilliant surgeon with little to no empathy. I had no problem deciding who I wanted at the operating table after that. I knew in my heart that I wanted someone who believed in our hope no matter how slim the chances. I also was adamant that whoever would be in the room with us at birth would be someone with compassion for our grieving hearts. Thus, we went back to the naval hospital to share our confidence in our own doctor, all the more appreciative for his down-to-earth character.

That summer, our pastor had started a new sermon series about the power of prayer. He was challenging us to spend the next thirty days building a "keystone habit" every morning by starting the day in quiet time. This pastor had made a point to remind us that when we pray about our needs, it is okay to ask for what we want, but in the end, we ultimately want to be seeking God's will for our lives. With Isaac, I constantly prayed for a miracle of healing, but in my heart, I knew that God had a beautifully laid-out plan for his life no matter what the outcome. I started praying for our baby's journey to shape us as believers and lead us to meet other parents in similar situations who were in need of encouragement. When I went looking for support, I had witnessed firsthand the gap of resources. Now it became clear that I had the background to add my voice to this difficult conversation.

In light of our desire to be surrounded by community, we made the bold decision to move from our little rental in Norfolk to a condo neighboring another wonderful couple who were leading our Bible study. Dan was a chief in the Navy, and his wife, Jennifer, was a nurse. Along with their two young children, they quickly became even closer friends as we traded football and barbeque nights at their house in exchange for my getting to babysit their little ones on occasion. When you are in the military and are far away from those you love, neighbors like these didn't get any better. It also never hurt to have a buddy in the Navy for Andrew to commiserate with and a nurse friend for me who could ease my mind when I had new-mom questions.

There is no doubt in my mind that God led me to start getting to know two other military wives from church who were also going through complicated pregnancies. I was one of the last of my college and California friends to get married, so I had missed out on hearing most of the common motherhood reflections. Still, none of them had ever talked about anything other than healthy babies. I would learn after the fact that a few people I knew had gone through miscarriages, and some also shared their fertility issues. I started to see the silencing shame that hovers like a fog over couples trying to start families and not having it happen perfectly on the first try. I was horrified that people I counted friends hadn't been able to talk about these tough subjects because they didn't know how to bring it up or who to talk to. I was determined to change this narrative.

I like to think that because I was so open with our church about the struggles we were having with a complex pregnancy, women took note that I might be someone they could confide in. My friend Bethany was the first such mom, who came over shortly after our meal train had been set up to deliver dinner for us. I invited her into our three-story condo, and we walked up the flight of stairs to our living and dining room. She made small talk for a bit about how things were going with Isaac before she shared that she and her husband, Chad, had just learned that their unborn baby girl had a very serious condition that would require open-heart surgery. I moved to hug her tightly in the middle of our kitchen. This was her third pregnancy, and I couldn't imagine what it was like having to go home to take care of her older two kids while carrying around the weight of the world. All I wanted to do most days was stay curled up in bed, snuggling my cat and watching romantic comedies that gave me an excuse to cry in the middle of the day. I silently made a commitment in my heart to make sure that she had someone she could check in with every day about doctor appointments, child-care needs, help cleaning house, or whatever other practical things I could do. The tables had turned, and I paused to consider what had been the kindest supports I had received thus far and tried to figure out how I could pay it forward.

Watching how she and Chad handled their baby journey as seasoned parents was a thing of awe. Bethany continued to donate her gifts and her beautiful voice to our worship and connect-team each Sunday, reaching out to people through the coffee cart at mid-week prayer and bringing meals to others who were going through hard things. I will never forget how she managed to keep loving her other two young kids amidst everything else she had going on. Somewhere in there, I remember Chad spending hours in his garage laboring over a homemade wooden bunk bed for his older children. One day, Bethany shared with me how her son had been praying for Isaac every night before bed and was getting so excited to meet him.

There is no right way to go through a time of uncertainty and doubt about things we don't have control over, but Bethany had a unique strength that gave me encouragement in my own journey. I had been searching online for encouragement and calling around town for support. But here, God was answering my prayer with friends who could walk alongside me even more presently physical.

Marisa arrived at Wednesday prayer one night and came over to talk to Bethany and me at the coffee bar as we waited for the service to begin. She confided that her latest ultrasound and pregnancy testing had come back positive for Down syndrome characteristics. She had been going in with her husband, Andy, for follow-ups, just like Andrew and I had, and we talked about what to expect. Later, they learned that just like Bethany and Chad, their child would also need open-heart surgery after birth. Marisa is the opposite of me in every way when it comes to worry. She and Andy tackled the news with pure grace and acceptance and began their own blog to educate people on Down syndrome. They turned it into an opportunity to find the ability in disability and the possible in impossible. Marisa is an incredibly caring soul who trusts God so fully with her heart that it helped me lean on Him even more when bouts of anxiety overwhelmed me.

These friendships got me thinking about forming a mothers' prayer group. I enlisted the help of a well-seasoned woman in our church who had raised five beautiful young adults, who all had equally big servant hearts that they dedicated to helping at our church. Mama Pitt, as she was known, along with one of her daughters, Ruth, helped me facilitate a book club. We started with Stormie Omartian's *The Power of a Praying Parent*. The group was a mix of women who were first-time moms and others who could give us insight into parenthood. Most of this second group of women I knew fairly well, since I was the face welcoming their families to children's church every Sunday. Other new moms, I was meeting for the first time. It was the perfect blend of personalities to all bring a little piece of wisdom, humor, and new friendship to the table. In a weird way, our first get-together served as a kind of baby shower, with prayers, encouragement, and support, rather than physical gifts. I didn't want a lot of baby things that would go to waste if we never got to bring Isaac home, so I didn't get the experience of having a birthing party.

I did, however, get to bond with Marisa in our third trimesters of pregnancy when we went consignment shopping for our firstborn boys. This became one of our many traditions as our friendship and bellies grew. I was looking specifically for shirts that buttoned at the neck so that we could safely get newborn clothes on Isaac in the hospital. We were both looking for things to pack our hospital bags with, in anticipation of long stays in the neonatal intensive care unit (NICU). Because of the parallels of our stories, especially Marisa's unborn son needing to have major surgery after birth, we were able to share advice on everything from choices of hospitals and doctors, to pregnancy cravings and those nasty sciatic nerve pains. More importantly, we shared what was in our hearts about the faith that we had in God, that He could bring our boys through and provide them with miraculous healing.

After one of our many outings together, I was updating my blog with the latest pregnancy journal entry. A dear friend of mine from California, who subsequently became the artist behind my cover of this book, wrote a lovely philosophical response that nailed the sentiment to many conversations I had had with Marisa.

> That's so wonderful, Laura. Even though any-thing can happen still, that is so encouraging. I'm glad God visibly is giving you what you need for each moment. Do you remember the McKenzie Study Center at the Gutenburg College in Oregon run by my father-in-law's friends that I'm sure I've told you about? I've been listening to David Crabtree's talks on Genesis. Every story

is about man being rebellious against God and not trusting Him to take care of our own needs, which leads him to do various things that God deals with in different ways, such as the flood, but as we see, even the flood and threat of punishment does not change man's rebellious ways. So God takes a different approach to man starting with Abram, an everyday man who he takes out of the city into the farmland and then into the wilderness in order to BUILD into him faith. God brings Abraham through a series of events that build into him a faith that recognizes God as one, as real, and as one who can be trusted with Abraham's own well-being so he, in turn, can focus on taking care of others, building this faith and communication with him over and over and over so that by the time Abraham is asked to do the hardest thing—kill his own child—he doesn't hesitate. Which blows me away. And even then, God provides a way out. In this way, I think, it's that much more lovely that you have named your son Isaac. God is building into you the faith and trust in Him so that when He asks you to do the hardest things—be it a decision about doctors or surgery or trusting God for Isaac's health or giving up your own comfort for your child— you will be where you need to be, with the right amount of resources and knowledge and faith and trust for that moment. So I hope for that to be encouraging. God has a plan and is building you both into who He needs you to be for His plan and for that child.

Much love and hugs,
Cindy

Like Cindy, whom I met as a camp counselor at the Christian camp Mount Hermon in the Santa Cruz mountains, Marisa was someone that I turned to for spiritual reading recommendations. She was involved in a variety of different Bible studies and had a stack of Christian literature that she would read alongside of her Bible quiet time each day. I have always struggled in this area, in part from having been a workaholic for much of my young adult life. Also, because I didn't have the best patience and dedication to form such committed habits. I admired these friends and was thankful for their sharing of wisdom with me in what they were learning.

Chapter 8

But those who hope in the Lord will renew their strength.
They will soar on wings like eagles, they will run and
not grow weary, they will walk and not be faint.

—Isaiah 40:31

As I neared my nine-month mark of pregnancy, I felt like it was time to take our "call to faith" on Isaac's testimony to a wider range of people in our church. Every Wednesday night at Upward Church, we had a prayer evening called *Refuel*, and I was given the opportunity to speak on one such occasion. I am not particularly fond of public speaking, but my heart for sharing and encouraging allows me to overcome my stage fright more often than not. Also, it was a way for me to update our church community one final time before our pending due date. I opened that night with a shout-out to our pastor's daughter for introducing me to my favorite strength song, "Come to Me," by Jenn Johnson from Bethel Music.

This song reminds me of why I love the analogy of a lighthouse, not only because of its connection with the Navy and bringing my husband home safely but also for its clear depiction of how I see God leading us through troubled waters. He calls us to safety in His light, to come ashore and fall into His open arms. Even now, when I listen to the song years later, as a mother, it can be sung to our own children as a prayer, promising them that God will remain steady and strong.

In the days that came, I relied heavily on the podcast that was produced of my talk. It was almost like I was giving myself my own pep talk as I listened, with reminders of holding onto hope that whatever might come was something that God would see us through. In our little moment in time, just five short months of living through such despair in Isaac's diagnosis, it was such a larger life lesson to rely on the belief that God is bigger than anything we are going through. There was nothing left for me to do to prepare. I had taken all the obligatory prenatal classes and read through *What to Expect When You're Expecting* by Heidi Murkoff. I had my hospital go-bag packed with various items that were on the recommended list in my little purple Navy pregnancy journal. In the bag, I also included things that I thought I would need for the longer NICU stay; I had already toured the floor and met our delivery team. I had a small fireman-print baby blanket, a few sailor-themed burp cloths, a nursing pillow, and the tiny newborn onesie I had optimistically settled on as Isaac's coming-home outfit. Now it was time to love on my husband and cherish our last few weeks of being a family of two before our lives were changed forever.

This included an incredible complimentary photo session by the renowned Hampton Roads photographer Bob Harper, to whom we had been referred though Edmarc Children's Hospice. Andrew and I drove up the coast to Fort Monroe, where we enjoyed a nice dinner date before meeting Bob on the beach at sunset. A former military man himself, Bob is well known in the community for providing his photography services to local charities. When we first spotted Bob in the parking lot, he was dressed in a floppy fishing hat and cargo shorts. He looked as though he could have been there on a bird watch to photograph the local flora and fauna. He had an easy nature about him in his casual look, and he quickly became a friend during our photo shoot. Bob was incredibly kind hearted as we smiled solemnly for pictures that may have been the only things documented from our Isaac pregnancy. He even invited us back later that week for an in-studio session to capture my bare belly and Andrew in his uniform.

I decided that I didn't want a fresh 48 photo-op that the hospital offered, where an in-house photographer came to document the early hours of a baby's arrival. I wasn't sure what the first few hours after Isaac's birth would be like, or what his head would look like for that matter. I wanted to control what photos were taken of him in such an intimate first meeting. It was really special to have the beautiful pregnancy portraits as a memento of our late days of pregnancy. I had been working with our Edmarc social worker Britney in those weeks as well to come up with other ideas for our birth plan. The hospice agency gave us a clay-kit frame to capture Isaac's footprints in the NICU. We talked about our birth plan and how to write up the important things we wanted to happen after my scheduled C-section. While there were some things we definitely couldn't choose, such as a natural birth due to the risk it presented to Isaac's enlarged head and birth defect, other things, like Andrew's part after the birth, were really important to me.

I knew that I would only have a brief first look after my C-section before Isaac would be whisked away to the NICU to be treated. I didn't want Andrew to miss any moments with our newborn baby, especially since I would be in recovery for a while. We agreed that he should cut the cord and take part in our baby's first bath, if possible, giving Andrew the opportunity to spend as much time as possible with Isaac in and around whatever medical attention he needed. We wanted the Navy chaplain to be there in the waiting room to pray over Isaac when he got to the NICU. And we wanted Andrew's parents there for support as well. I warned our friends and family that we might not update everyone at a moment's notice, thereby setting boundaries for us to be allowed to cope with whatever happened in a space that gave us the time we needed. I started my self-care mode of taking alone time and detaching from the hard questions of how I was doing and whether there was anything I needed. Our church family rallied behind us in prayer and sent us off after the service on Sunday with their final well-wishes before our Wednesday birth.

Andrew always joked that it took forever for us to get out of church on a normal Sunday, between people asking me questions about church nursery, talking to newcomers, and generally catching up with friends or trying to make plans for the week. This time though, we hung onto every handshake and hug that we got from the church pews as the last song played us out, to the final waves as we drove out of the parking lot.

Chapter 9

For you created my inmost being; you knit me together in my mother's womb. I praise you because I am fearfully and wonderfully made.
—Psalm 139:13–14

On August 14, I woke up to celebrate my thirty-first birthday and say a quick prayer with Andrew before we headed to Portsmouth Naval Hospital. He kissed me goodbye after the doctors gave us the all clear that the operating room was ready for the planned C-section. I had never been awake in an OR before, despite having had a surgery in the past. I felt like I was on a TV set before all the action took place as I sat in the cold room in my gown and hair cap watching all the surgical staff around me preparing. I didn't recognize any of them really. In the military, doctors typically work a four-week rotation, so aside from my neurosurgeon, I hadn't seen any of the staff before at my typical monthly checkups. They were as comforting as they could be considering the circumstances, but my empathetic side keyed in to their battle-ready faces, and I knew they were mentally preparing themselves for a medical emergency. I felt confident that this team had collaborated and knew their roles down to every last detail.

The nurse gave me an epidural in my spine, and I lay back on the hard metal operating table. I remember thinking that, at least, I wouldn't have to go through the pain and strain of natural childbirth on top of dealing with the emotional outcomes. I started silently going over my personal breathing exercise as they asked me if I could feel my toes. Be still (inhale)…and know that I am God (exhale)… over and over again until I had no sensation when they touched my stomach. They put the curtain up and the ventilation mask on. I was hooked up to a warmer, which puffed out my hospital gown with hot air like a sumo wrestler costume. I wasn't uncomfortable physically, but I was beginning to long for them to speed up the process so I could just meet Isaac. By this point, I was ready in my heart to say hello to my baby, no matter the outcome.

Andrew was in the OR with me by the time they started the surgery. He sat next to me so I could see him, and he wiped away each of my heartbroken tears as they began the first incision. If ever there was a model of strength in a man, Andrew fit the bill. He was stoic through it all, watching me, helplessly I am sure, as we both prayed life over our baby. When the doctors pulled Isaac out, Andrew was called over to cut the cord, and I heard his first cries to calm my anxious mommy heart. The doctors congratulated us quickly before getting Isaac's stats and wrapping him up for my first view of his beautiful face. I could hear the collective sigh of relief in the small room so full of people cheering for a miracle. I saw my little pink baby and gave him a kiss for our first family photo. Andrew was ushered out to meet Isaac in the NICU while they stitched me back up and sent me to the recovery room.

When I woke up from the anesthesia, it was like this maternal switch had been turned on and a magnetic force was pulling me toward my baby. I was so frustrated that I didn't have enough feeling back yet for them to be able to put me in a wheelchair and go to see Isaac. I was even more crazed wanting to know what had been going on medically while I was away from Andrew and Isaac, eager to learn how our little miracle fighter was doing. By the time I was wheeled in to the NICU, Andrew was sitting in the mauve patterned glider next to an empty crib space. He quickly told me that they had taken Isaac for an MRI of his brain. He went on to share that he had been able to give Isaac a bath and that the doctors were happy with how he was doing so far. The overall impression was the doctors didn't seem to think things were as bad as we had all anticipated. I met our NICU nurses and sat watching the door like a hawk for any sign of them wheeling a crib down the hall.

Finally, my beautiful boy arrived, looking so peaceful with his little head wrapped up in gauze. Outwardly, I could not see one scratch on his perfect body. Nothing was out of place, although I knew the cotton headdress was expertly hiding the imperfection in his brain. It didn't matter though because my sweet Isaac was alive. He didn't even seem to be in any pain or in need of too much extra support medically speaking. We were allowed to hold his tiny little hand with a finger through his Isolette. After some time, basking in the glory of being a family of three, we invited Andrew's parents to come in and meet their first grandchild.

The Hershey grandparents, as I like to call them, had flown out a few days earlier to celebrate August birthdays with a nice dinner out before the baby came. Both of them are physical therapists and have a relative comfort level for hospitals and medical talk. Although I am sure that no amount of experience could prepare them for the unknown in our situation, it nonetheless was nice to have family from California in town to support us. As much as I would have loved for my parents to be with their only child during delivery, I knew that my emotional bond with my mom would be a tearjerker in the final hour. We agreed instead that they would come out to celebrate our baby's first Christmas. I wasn't sure initially if I would want any visitors, even family, but it was sure nice to have the Hershey's on standby to give thanks for our miracle baby with relieved hugs.

We ended up texting our closest friends from church, campus pastor Tommy and his wife, Laura. We shared with them the happy news that Isaac had not only been born alive, but that the results of his MRI had come back with significantly less brain matter outside the skull than the doctors had thought. Additionally, Isaac was strong enough to go through removal surgery the following morning. That night happened to be Wednesday prayer at church, so we asked Tommy to share the details with our church family. After the service, they drove out to Portsmouth to visit us, and my heart was so grateful to share in that moment with our fellow prayer warriors.

Since Isaac wasn't able to feed or be held due to all the machines he had been hooked up to, I spent the night sleeping as best I could to recover for the long day of surgery ahead. The encephalocele itself was based at the back of the top of his head and was about the size of a large apricot. The doctors never actually showed us the deformation, for which I am thankful. In my research leading up to Isaac's birth, I had forced myself to look at pictures to take away the potential shock value. But our beautiful boy was a precious miniature version of his daddy from the get-go. I hadn't prepared myself for how hard it would be to watch the nurses wheel him away for surgery since we had been so busy guarding our hearts against the sadness we thought would come from anticipated hospice care. This was an entirely new challenge of emotions as parents with a heartstring attachment to this living, breathing baby boy.

Incredibly, Isaac came out of surgery with no complications, and the doctors closed up his head with a protective layer of skin that covered the empty gap in his skull. We still weren't able to hold him just yet, but I sat for hours staring at him in amazement that he was finally here and on the other side of surgery. I called our team at Edmarc, whose offices were just a few short blocks away, to share all the details and cried happy tears with them. I knew that we would need their nurses and social workers' support in the weeks ahead in the NICU and for Isaac's subsequent discharge. For now, I was thankful that the immediate threat to Isaac's well-being had passed.

In the days that followed, Marisa and her husband, Andy, toured the NICU as they prepared for their own birth story. I remember talking to my Andrew about these new friends whom he hadn't met yet. I told him that they were walking this unknown pregnancy journey with us, as well as our other friends Bethany and Chad, and I had hoped we could give them a peek at our little world. My protective instinct to keep Isaac just to ourselves was quickly replaced with wanting to give these friends of mine a tangible vision of hope through our testimony. While our birth story was taking on a new course in Isaac's life, it was still important to me that we didn't have our focus fall completely inward to the point where we forgot to continue to stand by these other two couples. It is so funny looking back on that time of our first visitors outside of the grandparents, the chaplain, and our campus pastor. God definitely was weaving our stories, our friendship, and our children together through an unforgettable modern-day miracle.

FACEBOOK STATUS:

Hello, world! Thanks for all your birthday and well-wishes. Isaac Bruce arrived 8/14 at 8:28 a.m. Went through brain surgery 8/15 and has been recovering well ever since. Diagnosis is much less severe than previously anticipated, so no shunt was installed at this time. 8/16 was our first hold and bottle feeds which will be progressing in frequency as Isaac is unplugged from his various tubing lines. I am being discharged today but will be on sleeper status tonight so that we can stay one more day close to the NICU. We have the option to stay on base at the Fisher House till Thursday as well. Mom and baby are getting stronger every day. :) Continued prayers for Isaac's brain to heal.

- Yay!!! It was great seeing you both and your little miracle yesterday!!!! :) We continue to pray for healing for you both! (Marisa)
- So awesome!!! :-D I have been anxiously awaiting this news all week—I knew God was going to show up and show out! (Chelsi)
- Praise God! You guys have been on my mind and in my prayers often. (Candace)
- I'm so happy for you guys. It's been an amazing week! (Tommy)
- Congrats, mama! Such good news! You have prayers from all over the world coming your way. Miss you guys! (Mahayley)

Chapter 10

Peace I leave with you; my peace I give you. I do not give to you as the world gives. Do not let your hearts be troubled and do not be afraid.
—John 14:27

Over the next few days, Isaac's healing progressed enough for us to move from tube nutrition feeding to the bottle, holding him for the first time, and an attempt at nursing. It was maternal torture to only get fifteen minutes an hour to snuggle my baby when all I wanted to do was to be a mama kangaroo and hold him skin-to-skin. But watching Andrew take his turn and embrace that initial daddy bonding was a magical experience in itself. Our family had a new sense of completeness to it. Andrew's dad flew home the day I was discharged from the hospital, but his mom was able to stay to support us in our upcoming transition home. The military allowed us to use their on-site family housing for long-term crisis care, the Fisher House on base. It is comparable to the Ronald McDonald houses that civilian hospitals have. Actually, I have never been inside one of these places, so all I had was the visual of the hospital-style hotel that I had seen in commercials.

The Fisher House was a beautiful brick building like you would find in a middle-class Virginia neighborhood. It had a classic Victorian elegance both inside and out. The hostess seemed more like a long-time bed-and-breakfast owner who would always have a pot of coffee and a tasty treat on the kitchen counter for us to enjoy. We were encouraged to use it as a home away from home, and I was thankful for the five-minute walk from the hospital rather than having to drive thirty minutes through bridge and tunnel traffic. The blessings that we were gifted with left and right were like the cherry on top. When the NICU staff told us we were likely to be looking at discharge just one week after surgery and, subsequently, Andrew's birthday, we went out to celebrate.

Sadly, that night we experienced our first setback when they realized Isaac's surgery site was leaking cerebral spinal fluid (CSF) and that he would need to go in for a second surgery to place a shunt to manage his hydrocephalus. Although we had been warned that this might happen, sending our one-week-old baby in for brain surgery again was devastating. We went through the motions again the next few days, waiting and watching to see Isaac stabilize, by this point, having also said goodbye to Andrew's mom and going back to our house to wait for discharge. Week two came with another failed attempt to leave the NICU when the shunt needed an emergency repair. That night, the hospital put us up in one of their mommy wards to be near Isaac before and after the surgery. I hated seeing him intubated and listening to his muted cries, but I hated even more having to go home without him. After a fever spike and concerns that they needed to do a fourth surgery to get Isaac stable, he had had enough and proved that his little body was fighting on its own for discharge. At nineteen days old, we took Isaac home to Virginia Beach.

When we arrived at our town house, we walked into a living room surprise: a hand-me-down bedside-reach crib filled with clothes and all sorts of baby things from our neighbors. In the weeks that followed, we couldn't go a day without our doorbell ringing, bringing friends delivering food, gifts, and hugs, in fair exchange to see our miracle baby and report back to our church community. Our mailbox, emails, and cellphones were equally filled with well-wishes and exclamations of praise and celebration of Isaac's birth and discharge home. We had strangers from all corners of the United States commenting on my blog with stories of their own that touched my heart in such a deep way to be able to walk this journey alongside so many.

It is not uncommon to start meeting people who hear our story and open up about what their own families have been through. The easiest way for me to explain this unique phenomenon is to compare it to when you are in the hunt for a new vehicle. Typically, while driving on the freeway, I will notice fancy cars if they are brightly colored and overly expensive. I might pause to notice the soccer mom van in the commercials I always see on TV. But generally, unless someone cuts me off in traffic, and I want to get a second look at the type of car the maniac is driving, I don't really pay too much attention to brand or style—that is, until I am in the market for a new car. Then all I do is see that exact car I have my eye on everywhere on the road. Old models and colors to the newest trims seem to be parked next to me in my neighbor's driveway or at the doctor's office. My mind's unconscious focus on buying this new car is now forefront to everything I observe around me.

Similarly, an entirely new world was opened to my eyes when I became a special-needs mom. If I had thought that I was comfortable with this population in the counseling and education world before, it was nothing compared to the realities that people shared now that they knew I had experienced it personally. In our frequent visits to the hospital for follow-up doctor appointments, we were no longer checking in and sitting by ourselves as we waited. New connections formed in the office waiting room as complete strangers bonded over the challenges of having to see these pediatric specialists. I began to be drawn to certain families in the community, at the park or grocery store or library. It was almost like I was being initiated into a secret club that I had been practically oblivious to before becoming a mom, but this was an even more super-elite club of special-needs parents.

I have learned so much in these last years from loving, watching, listening to, and learning about these beautiful children and their families. It is certainly a life-changing experience for each family going through their own unique story, and it is equally important to validate their difficulties and to celebrate their blessings. I have received text messages from acquaintances about new diagnoses their child just received. I have been pulled over discreetly at play groups and asked what local resources and therapies we have for Isaac. Often, I will get an email or a message on social media from friends asking if they can forward my information on to another friend of theirs who just got handed bad news. As much as I am grateful to be a resource for these families, it is the moms who confide in me about stories of pregnancy loss that I hold the most cherished. It is an honor to be given a glimpse at stories that are often untold, to be able to offer whatever I can to help lessen the load of that silent burden that these women carry.

Our closest friends, Marisa and Andy, are a family that has been with us since the beginning, often in the midst of the hardest parts. They were a fellow military couple we met at Upward Church, also new to Virginia and far from their families, who lived in the Midwest. Marisa was about two-and-a-half months behind me in pregnancy and found out their baby's diagnosis at their twenty-one-week checkup. Much like our story, they would go on to get more specifics about Beau's condition, some of which could be tested and others that were a wait-and-see sort of thing to determine the severity. When they found out that it was almost a certainty that Beau would have Down syndrome, Marisa shared in an early blog post about a story she had come across by Emily Perl Kingsley called "Welcome to Holland."

It speaks to planning a trip to Italy and all the beautiful things the author hopes to see and do. But on the plane there, it is announced that she is actually going to Holland. She is obviously frustrated and confused by this change in plans and feels totally unprepared to visit this other country. The moral of the story is that while her expectations were disappointed when she didn't go to Italy, as she adjusted to Holland, she was able to experience the amazing things that country had to offer.

This piece reminded me immediately of some of the articles I had come across in my research for my master's thesis. Mainly, they were stories shared by mothers going through the diagnosis of autism and how it dramatically shaped what they thought their child and family's future would look like. As you can imagine, many people experience shock and disbelief similar to what we went through. Many more grieve the life they dreamed their children would have, whether sports, education, relationships, or career. I read stories of fathers who had been star athletes in college and who had innocently bought their babies "little slugger" onesies or "MVP" hats, only to mourn the child's inability to play in traditional contact sports. Other times, there were memories of silly milestone graduations moms joked about that were plastered over Facebook, only to wish their own child could celebrate such little things as mastering potty training. Most of the time, though, I read the heartbreak of parents worrying that their children with special needs would be excluded from social events or, even worse, learning the child had been the target of bullying.

I admired our friends Marisa and Andy; I watched them lean in to God and believe that their baby was a gift from the Lord no matter what. If I thought that I had been the research queen about Isaac's diagnosis, these friends were on an equal level of not only understanding for themselves but educating friends and family through their blog and social media. It was encouraging to me to watch how Marisa handled setbacks by trusting God for Beau's healing rather than allowing worry and anxiety to overcome her thoughts. In one instance, they were presented with the choice to get a particularly risky test done to confirm whether or not Beau had Down syndrome. I will never forget Marisa's adamancy that they didn't need to have the test because it wouldn't change anything. Whether he did or did not was not going to affect their birth plan. In fact, she seemed to carry a quiet confidence that Beau didn't need to be "fixed" and was quick to point out all the positive traits people with Down syndrome tend to have, in particular, their often happy outlook on life. This did not mean that she was not experiencing sadness or nerves regarding his birth or potential heart surgery, but she carried a silent strength in her trust that God would see them through whatever might come.

Ultimately, Beau was born six weeks early and spent more than eighty days in the hospital before he was able to go home. Marisa and I became appointment buddies, sharing updates on what was happening with our baby boys, as well as which doctors we liked the best. We commiserated over the long drive to and from the hospital that included timing the bridge openings and avoiding the naval base workday that let out at 3:00 p.m. each day. We talked about the tricks to picking up prescriptions at the drive-through of the smaller pharmacy at Little Creek versus having to go to NMCP and deal with the longer waits at the Navy hospital. Together with our spouses, we started a Thanksgiving tradition where we spent the holiday together since the four of us were all equally far from our loved ones back home. The husbands, Andrew and Andy, bonded over a love of football, woodworking, and a shared military experience. We could not have asked for better friends to go through this baby journey with us had we put an ad on social media seeking special-needs parent support. When Beau graduated from the PICU and moved to the general pediatric floor we were excited for this long-awaited milestone. When he was discharged in early December, we celebrated that extra joy of our miracle babies all being at home in the festive Christmas season.

Chapter 11

So do not worry about tomorrow, for tomorrow will care
for itself. Each day has enough trouble of its own.
—Matthew 6:34

Isaac's first Christmas was a truly grand celebration as we hosted his nana and papa, my parents, for an East Coast winter wonderland. The festivities started early with a visit from the Edmarc Hospice Santa and his elves bringing their red bag filled with presents for the whole family. By the time the grandparents had arrived for their two-week visit, our Christmas tree barely had any room left underneath for gifts. I was eager to fill our family time with memories of the local festivities. We drove through the Norfolk Botanical Garden's holiday light show with Isaac bundled in a reindeer snowsuit and warmed up with a fancy Christmas Eve meal at the Founders Inn and Spa. The head chef attended our church and had told us to let him know when we arrived. After we had eaten one of the best meals of land and surf, our waiter brought out a full-size lineup of every dessert on the menu, compliments of the chef. Somehow, I managed to squeeze into my swimsuit afterward so that I could take Isaac for his first swim in the heated indoor hotel pool.

Back at our condo, my dad, or Papa, as he is known to my kids, built a firehouse bookshelf to match Isaac's nursery theme. Andrew had recently put together the mahogany bedroom set in anticipation of moving Isaac out of our room and the bedside crib. Isaac's nursery began to take shape with all the new firehouse bedding and other décor that he had been given. I couldn't help but cry happy tears every time we opened something that said "baby's first Christmas."

Our time with my parents flew by, and I realized just how much I had missed having them close and wished that someday we would all be back living on the same coast again. We rang in the New Year together before my mom and dad said their goodbyes. I had planned to take them to breakfast before driving them to the airport that day, but instead, we got our first true Isaac emergency. Over the previous twenty-four hours, I had noticed a slight shade of blue on Isaac's lips as he was falling asleep for naps. I thought he might be having some apnea and tried to change his position. He didn't seem to have any other symptoms other than these quick three-to-five-second blue episodes, until New Year's Day.

Isaac was in his glider swing, and I noticed that he was not reviving from the blue lips and had become nonresponsive to me trying to wake him up. I took him out of the swing, and he felt limp as I held him. My lifeguard instincts kicked in, and I did rescue breathing until he opened his eyes. I packed up the diaper bag and took him to the closest emergency room. The five-minute drive felt like five hours as I rushed through the neighborhood, hoping he wouldn't lose consciousness in the back seat. At every stoplight, I would tap him and talk to him, praying that he would stay awake long enough for me to get to the ER. When I finally arrived, I rushed into the waiting room to find two people standing in front of me at the check-in desk. As I frantically paced waiting my turn, Isaac started to turn blue again. I started to panic at this point and shouted to the nurse that my baby couldn't breathe. I remember the nice gentleman in front of me coming over to take my bag as the hospital staff moved us directly into a curtained area. They gave Isaac oxygen, and he came around easily. But as we waited to be admitted into the back, he had another blue event and still another when we got to our single room. The staff quickly got on the phone to Norfolk Children's Hospital to get us an ambulance transport to Portsmouth Naval Hospital.

I called Andrew at work and told him to meet us on base. When we arrived there, they took us up to the PICU, and our neurosurgery team descended on us within the hour. Over the next four days, the doctors ran every test they could think of. Everything seemed stable in their opinion, but he was still having blue episodes with relative frequency. The short EEG they ran, however, didn't catch any of the abnormal activity. Running out of options, they decided to do an overnight test to see if a longer EEG would capture anything. During the eight hours of monitoring, Isaac had ten blue events. At one point, the doctor told the nurses not to give him oxygen to see if he could recover on his own and how long it would take.

It was completely traumatizing to watch my four-month-old baby struggling to breathe as a room full of specialists looked on doing nothing. I stood in the background, leaning against the large glass sliding doors that separated our spacious private room from the nurses' desk just across the way. Isaac was hooked up to just as many cords and machines as he had been when he got out of brain surgery. The nurse stood by the emergency oxygen in her green scrubs while the doctors and surgeons stood out in shades of light and dark blue. The on-call specialist from our birth team wore civilian clothes: jeans and a black Patagonia zip-up. I am sure I looked like a hot mess after having stayed up on New Year's Eve and not gotten caffeine or a shower before we ended up in the hospital.

Andrew and I took turns spending the night at the hospital in hopes that the other could get some sleep in between the long days. As we would come back together each morning, we could see the results of each other's trauma and despair from the previous night's struggle. The noise from the pulse oxygen machine when Isaac lost consciousness was loud and alarming as the team rushed in to give him oxygen. But the blood draws were the absolute worst. Andrew and I tried not to detail the horror stories of having to hold down our screaming baby while the nurses tried to find a vein that hadn't been blown. It was cruel and unusual punishment to have to put Isaac through that much more pain. Both of us agreed that this stay in the PICU was far worse than any part of Isaac's birth story or subsequent time in the NICU.

During my pregnancy, we knew what the likely outcome of Isaac's diagnosis would be. Our doctors had a pretty firm idea of what was going on and what our options were. We didn't know how bad things would be at birth, but we had prepared ourselves for the worst. This time around, the doctors had no clue what was going on.

They seemed to be just as helpless as we felt, standing back watching and waiting for answers. Eventually, it was confirmed that Isaac's blue spells were actually seizures, and we added the neurologist in attendance to our team. I don't know that we were relieved per se. I was thankful that we had an idea of what we were dealing with now, but on the other hand, seizures felt much more uncontrollable on a day-to-day basis. I was overwhelmed by the thought of leaving Isaac alone for even a minute to go to the bathroom, let alone be in a separate from him to sleep an entire night.

When Isaac was finally discharged, we picked up our prescription for his new seizure meds and contacted Edmarc for support. Our Navy doctor team had recommended that we try to get a home oxygen tank for him as well as a pulse-ox monitor to keep an eye on him as he slept. This was one of many times that Edmarc came to the rescue when regular health care couldn't get things approved for us in a timely manner, if at all. We had both of our requested items delivered to our house within twenty-four hours. On more than one occasion, I thanked my lucky stars when I called the Edmarc nurse line in the middle of the night with a concern and heard a friendly and familiar voice on the other end calming my fears. The next day, someone from the agency would always show up in person as an added bonus of follow-up support. Since Isaac had initially come home from the hospital, Edmarc had moved from once-a-week visits down to bi-monthly visits as he stabilized. Now they were back to our more frequent support meetings, and I was ever so thankful to have them as an extra set of eyes to check on Isaac.

I am pretty sure I didn't sleep the entire month of January as we adjusted to life with a baby who had a new epilepsy diagnosis. Friends of mine would occasionally come over to hang out while I took a catnap, just to offer me a breath of respite. I also invested in a bouncer chair to keep in the bathroom so that I felt that Isaac would be within a safe distance from me in case of emergency.

It seemed like my worry was valid as Isaac experienced his first breakthrough seizures just three weeks later. We went back to the neurologist for an increase of medication and came home with our hawk eyes even more closely watching him.

Around this same time, as our family was settling back in at home, Marisa and Andy were making decisions on Beau's upcoming open-heart surgery. Marisa and I had become fierce prayer warriors for each other and advocates for speaking up for various medical services that we needed. We would share text messages of prayers on mornings we knew the other was going in to various appointments and check in late at night to offer support after long days. Again, I was blown away by the strength our friends showed in the face of such difficult times and encouraged by their faith in all circumstances. Beau's surgery was a success, but the complications that followed with the variety of his other health needs were often just as tough.

One thing that I learned from watching them go through these medical issues both big and small was just how challenging the stubborn daily battles could be. Between Beau's need for a feeding tube, around-the-clock oxygen, and a smattering of other surgeries that came up, there was a constant revolving door of doctors' appointments and hospital stays that Marisa and Andy attended to keep Beau healthy. It was during mommy visits that I began to see the toll it was taking on our families for all these other medical needs our boys had. While Isaac's brain surgeries and Beau's heart surgery were obviously major risky events, it often felt harder dealing with all the additional medical challenges that our boys were going through. Surgery itself was very defined, while the rest of the things going on had no definite healing date. There was so much unknown in what to expect, and the adjustments that needed to be made to accommodate for their health in daily activities outside the house took some getting used to.

Beau and Isaac were both still firmly in the medically fragile category. Neither of our families were supposed to make unnecessary trips past driving to doctors' appointments. Grocery store runs and trips to Target for diapers aside, going to places like church where large groups of people and germs lingered was highly discouraged. With Isaac's thin layer of skin as the only covering between his brain and the outside world, he was particularly susceptible to the threat of meningitis. Beau, with his weak immune system, easily caught colds, which complicated his breathing even further. It was a vicious cycle to keep our boys healthy when we had to make trips to the hospital where we knew so many sick people were passing us in the halls.

Isaac celebrated his half-birthday on Valentine's Day and consistently checked off his well-baby milestones in amazing fashion. He was rolling over back-to-belly and vice versa, sitting up on his own unassisted, and even had six teeth by six months. The last week of March, Andrew and I reminisced about the diagnosis day from the previous year and wondered in awe at the miracle of Isaac's health and stability that the doctors never imagined he would live to see. By his nine-month checkup, Isaac was on the fence with some feeding and crawling skills for his age. We got some preliminary referrals for assessment with a few specialists in the hospital. I distinctly remember sitting down during an intake with a potential feeding therapist to talk about what we saw as challenges or needs, along with the strengths and goals we had for Isaac. My response to this woman and many more after her was always the same. I felt so strongly about how many diagnosis prognoses Isaac had overcome that I was just thankful for how strong he was.

As new parents, we might have easily chalked this up to not knowing what skills a baby should have by various ages. But for me, I celebrated all that Isaac had accomplished in his short life thus far. He was the happiest baby on the block, and stable. Beyond that, I really had no complaints. As each new referral came in, and I met with another new therapist, my goals for him remained the same: give him the time and space to get the next thing in his own way and watch him thrive in the meantime. Isaac was inquisitive and loved to try to manipulate objects to see how they worked. I wasn't worried that he couldn't get the triangle into the shape sorter. He was also very observant and loved to sit and watch the people around him in a room. It didn't matter to me that he army-crawled on his belly with effort rather than power crawling to get to where he was going. Isaac also proved to anyone who looked at him that he was well fed on his milk diet of half breastfeeding and half baby formula. His chunky cheeks showed that he was not missing out on solid foods just yet. Andrew and I were perfectly okay to let Isaac go at his own pace.

During my quest to get involved with the special-needs community and meet other families going through a similar situation as ours, I stumbled upon an organization called Faith Inclusion Network. I attended an event they were hosting, in hopes of networking with some of the people. The speaker was an author who told her story of raising a child with severe autism. It was nice to hear some familiar things in how she coped with special-needs parenthood, but I also selfishly wondered if I would find other people who were experiencing the types of medical uncertainty Isaac's diagnosis gave us. This was and still is a recurring thought I have after every group I participate in. I don't feel like we are worse off by any means, and really, when I think of something like autism, I know the questions parents have about their kids' future are equally significant. I guess I just selfishly wish I had more information on how to best care for my child who's very being, at the brain level, was never fully formed. I wish I had a better parenting guide that went past the massive zero-to-five milestone book that I pored over in attempts to grasp how to give my child what his uniquely individual mind and body needed.

Despite all these thoughts, after the speaker was done, I introduced myself to the director who had sponsored the event. She assured me that there would be a place for me and Isaac's story in another group of women who were involved in a moms' support group at a local church. I called Marisa about it and invited her to join me a few months later at the first get-to-know-you event. The group had been formed out of common diagnoses in a local church that was providing special-needs buddies to their kids. These moms formed the foundation, and from there, word of mouth spread. As we started to brainstorm about what we were looking for and how to reach others in the area, we came up with the name "Living in Holland" as a tribute to the essay that was significant to each of us, and how we wanted to walk alongside one another on this oft foreign adventure. Ultimately, it reminded me that we were all looking for a place to share the hard times and to see the understanding looks and nods from other moms who were dealing with so much more than the everyday common trials of parenthood that are already hard enough.

Over the next year, this group of women came together once a month to talk about books we had read in the special-needs world, to share resources with one another, and to commiserate over medical challenges and school concerns. But mostly, we were there for one another in-between, offering friendship and nods of understanding or prayers on Facebook posts. I think the group description explains our purpose best: "Raising a child with special needs takes an extraordinary amount of time, energy, and expense. Often, as caregivers, we neglect taking care of ourselves, spending all of our time tending to the needs of our child with special needs and to the rest of the family. Living in Holland meetings are an opportunity to spend some relaxed time with other moms who understand our unique challenges." A few years down the road, I would come to learn that similar villages exist in the foster-care community. In both cases, I have witnessed the importance of walking the journey alongside one another and being in the midst of it all together.

During that summer, our family also began looking for a new church home to help meet the needs of providing a safe Sunday school environment for Isaac. My "Living in Holland" friends were a great resource to help us check out places that might be a good fit. Ultimately, we landed at Grace Virginia Beach, where we were immediately able to plug Isaac in with a buddy. Here also, I made steps to get involved and learn about their special-needs ministry and about what it takes to make a program successful and what I could do to help spread this mission.

By this time, I had decided to be a full-time, stay-at-home mom, and I was eager to put my social work counseling background to good use. Looking back, each of these experiences was a guidepost that served to help me know how to advocate for Isaac in the future. What a truly incredible blessing our time in Virginia was in all of the ways it taught me things about the special-needs world. Even more so, blogging our adventures and activities allowed me to look back on things and see just how far we had come, not just in growth milestones and parenting but in life lessons and bearing witness to God's continued faithfulness.

Chapter 12

*Now faith is confidence in what we hope for and
assurance about what we do not see.*

—Hebrews 11:1

As we prepared to celebrate Isaac's first birthday, we flew to Southern California to meet the extended Hershberger family. There is something about having kids that makes you wish you could raise your family surrounded by loved ones. Introducing Isaac to his great-grandma, aunts, uncles, and cousins sure planted the homesick bug. Andrew's grandmother, or Gigi, as she is affectionately called, scanned a copy of a picture of Isaac in a firefighter outfit and put it on his birthday cake. The entire extended Hershey family sang to him as Andrew and I blew out his single candle. My favorite photo from that trip is one of Isaac in his namesake Uncle Bruce's arms. They have the same sandy-colored hair with shades of strawberry blond as well as the very dominant male Hershberger squint. We took Isaac to see the Pacific Ocean and the attached local park. We slowly meandered down many beach piers and basked in the salty air and gentle breeze. After a few glorious days of surf and sand, we hopped on another plane to fly north to our previous hometown near Sacramento.

My in-laws hosted a giant August birthday celebration for our fourteenth-day trio: my mother-in-law, Isaac, and me, as well as Andrew on the twenty-first. My heart burst watching my extended family meet Isaac and see the smiling face of our miracle boy in person. Many of our dedicated prayer warriors stopped in to say hello, and the tug on our hearts to move home felt even stronger. Extended family members drove two hours to visit, and a group came from our Bible study that we had been a part of before we got married. The most surprising face there was one of my in-law's neighbors, who also happened to have been my youth pastor in junior high. I hadn't seen him in years, and he had no idea that I was the daughter-in-law whose baby he and his wife had been praying for over the past year. This was just one of many full-circle moments where we saw how far our story had traveled. Looking around at this village of people I knew so well, it was time to share a new prayer request. Andrew and I announced our second pregnancy and our hope that this group of friends and family would come alongside us again to pray for a healthy baby.

Such a complicated mix of emotions surrounded our announcement. Internally, I wanted to hide this baby growing inside of me until the doctors could confirm everything would be okay. But Isaac had taught me that no matter what might come, things would be okay anyway. Andrew and I decided to bring those closest to us into our news early so that we could feel that love and support they were so good at building us up with. Our fragile parent hearts were anxious about whether baby number two would have any health concerns as the doctors had previously told us there would be a higher probability that this could happen again. If I had thought waiting for Isaac's birth was nerve-wracking, the anticipation of our first ultrasound the second go-round was equally stressful.

However, this time, I had a sweet toddler underfoot to remind me that life is all around us, and there just isn't time to stop and sit still to worry very long. Things in Virginia were picking up as Isaac's therapies became more frequent. It is still an incredible thing to me that this entire world of at-home specialists came to our door each week and provided support on such a wide range of the needs we had. Early intervention is, by far, the biggest thing I like to advocate for to any new parent friends who have concerns about their children's development. When we got to attend the Naval Hospital's NICU reunion in September, I couldn't help but think that our kids had such a unique group of team members watching out for them—from the incredible group of nurses and doctors who brought our babies into the world and celebrated their going home, to the hand-off to the pediatric group of specialists who would take over from there, and on to outside referrals with community agencies and, eventually, the graduation into the school-district services. There are many challenges in navigating access to all that is available or to advocate for what should be offered, but when you find the right group, it is an awesome thing to watch your child thrive.

Edmarc Hospice was one agency that had been with us since the very beginning. After more than a year of their providing home nursing services and drop-in social work visits to see how they could support us, we began to talk about getting a healthy discharge for Isaac. When we had first been introduced to Edmarc's services, they made it clear that we would have their support indefinitely. I had no doubt that we would always be able to call them if we needed anything, but they went above and beyond basic availability and truly made us feel like we were just as important as any of their other kiddos struggling with life-threating conditions.

Early one morning, when Isaac had his longest seizure to date at close to one hour, all talk of discharge was put on the back burner, and they stepped right back in to more frequent house calls. One of the particularly troubling things about this breakthrough seizure was that the symptoms had changed. Instead of the blue lips and loss of consciousness, Isaac had gone limp while crawling during play. Then I noticed his leg had started to twitch. After I called 911, and they reached the house, the twitching had moved up to his arm also. Even when emergency seizure meds were given, no relief came, and I watched the twitch jump to the other side of his body. Things were getting serious as I watched the EMTs try everything available to them, but with no luck. At the children's hospital, our next battle began as the staff struggled to get an IV started to give him more direct medication. The trauma that flooded back from our hospital stay and initial round of seizures at the beginning of the year exploded into an even more intense fear for our boy's life.

I tried my best to hold it together while they called in the steadiest hands to attempt the IV. I explained that Isaac was a tough stick, and that in previous hospital stays, we literally had to hold him down while the nurses tried. The staff could see the pain in my eyes as I hugged my boy tightly and tried helplessly to calm him in-between each try to find a good vein. Eventually, they brought in an ultrasound machine and found an appropriate line in, but not without leaving a trail of bruised attempts in his arms. Isaac cried himself hoarse after the debacle, and I cradled him in his fireman blanket as he sucked on his favorite pacifier with the green frog attached to it.

After about four hours, Isaac was stable enough to transfer from the Children's Hospital to our PICU at the Naval Hospital, where his team was on standby. I remember the worried looks on the floor doctor's face as we came in and wondered why the seizures had changed so drastically and where to go from there. They kept him overnight to watch how a secondary med would work to keep him from having any more breakthroughs. They discharged him after around thirty-six hours, and we went home to try to rest, but by that same night, we were back in the emergency room after Isaac had a severe allergic reaction to the new medication. Not only did he experience severe face swelling and hives on the rest of his body, but the dose left our boy in a cognitive depression for close to two weeks without smiling. Isaac would look at Andrew and me with an expressionless face, almost as if he had no recognition of us, even though he hated it when we were out of eyesight. He cried more than usual and was difficult to comfort, and when he slept, I worried that he wouldn't wake up again. Our joyful boy, the embodiment of his name Isaac (meaning laughter), had really been hit hard by the brain recovery it took to get him back to normal, and my poor mama's heart and pregnant emotions were spiraling.

It was no coincidence then that just weeks later, I would be reflecting on the influence Edmarc had thus far had on our lives. A few months previously, they had asked if I would be willing to speak at their annual fundraiser breakfast and share our Isaac testimony. For a verbal processer like myself, it was such a sweet opportunity to look back on all the things we had overcome in Isaac's medical journey. Also, what a true honor it was to be able to thank them all in such a public way for the support Edmarc had provided our family from birth till then. They also arranged for a videographer to come to interview us alongside our nurse and social worker to show at another annual event they had coming up. This charity gala lived up to its hype, and Andrew and I got dressed up in black tie and a floor length gown to attend a swanky beachside event hall at Fort Monroe. As we sat in the dimly lit ballroom, I admired all of the people in attendance and thought about what another incredible moment we had to have Isaac's story told and to share Edmarc's part in it. It was wonderful to put it out into the community, for others to be encouraged about what their financial support was doing to get families in need of children's hospice the services they deserved.

Not only did Edmarc support us medically with nurses, social workers, and home health equipment but also through various referrals. In November, Isaac had a more severe breakthrough seizure that left us uncertain how to help him. At the time, the primary doctor who sat on Edmarc's board of directors was also the clinical director and top neurologist at our local children's hospital. Quite the busy guy, Dr. Northam was also a big name in the Virginia political scene at the time, so getting an office appointment with him was tricky. Somehow, Edmarc worked their magic again, and we were able to see the doctor in less than a month to get a second opinion on the medications Isaac was taking.

At that office visit, I learned just how important it was to work with doctors who speak the truth in love and to appreciate meeting brilliant people at the top of their fields whose best practice focused on client-centered work. I was wary from my experience with the children's hospital neurosurgeon we had met the previous year, but I knew that this neurologist came with a charity recommendation. When Andrew and I walked into the waiting room with Isaac, the warm, colorful décor stood in stark contrast to the aging halls of the grey concrete Navy hospital. We waited barely five minutes before being ushered back by the specialist himself. He greeted us warmly and took Isaac from me in a familial gesture. He gave off good vibes that reminded me of our Navy neurosurgeon we admired. Dr. Northam shared with us that the field of pediatric neurology could be considered one of the most difficult as there is no standard version in reading EEGs when it comes to such young children's brains that are still forming at such a high rate of growth and development. Also, every doctor has his or her trusted go-to medications and recommendations they give for such treatment. Essentially, what I took away was that we needed to find someone we believed in and could listen to in our gut as parents to continue to advocate for Isaac's care. I felt like this was an important turning point for any advice I got that I would hold strong to in the future.

It was incredibly challenging for me to feel that I could be a good parent to a child whose medical issues were so far above my scope of knowledge and capabilities. As a social worker, I spent hours looking for available resources and the best options for my kid. But it is tough to know when to keep pushing, to keep advocating for different kinds of care when I am interacting with brain surgeons. Yet time and time again, I found myself going back to the fact that we are Isaac's parents. Andrew and I know him best. I can tell his hurt cries from his hungry cries and even anticipate when an environment will be a sensory overload trigger. We have to give ourselves credit that we are capable of taking care of our kids by asking for what they need and not giving up until we get what is necessary for them to thrive. I remember laughing out loud when I saw a social media meme that said, "I'm not really a mama bear, I'm more of a mama llama. Like, I'm pretty chill, but I'll kick you in the face if you screw with my kids." Crude humor aside, the sentiment sticks. I am not the kind of social worker who will go door-to-door for my cause or stand on my soap box in public, nor will I have the loudest voice in the town hall meeting, but I am the kind of person who will do all the leg work of making calls and spending hours on hold and even more time surfing the internet for contact information to find the people who can make things happen. More importantly, I am the kind of person who won't give up on my cause until I have spoken face-to-face with someone and made sure my voice is heard. No future doctorate degree I pursue would change what I can do in the here and now.

Chapter 13

Be who God meant you to be and you will set the world on fire.
—St. Catherine of Siena

With my fierce mama heart and well-earned life lessons in tow, I still went into my five-month pregnancy checkup with my teeth gritted and my hands clenched in anticipation of the news. At our three-month ultrasound, the neonatal specialist had found concerning measurements in the baby's brain. It felt like an all-too-familiar story, and over the next eight weeks, I had to find every way possible to get myself out of the house and distracted in order to avoid thinking about all the potential problems we might be facing again. Every day, I forced myself to make plans with Marisa or Christy for the week, and in between, I called my mom and close friends from back home frequently. This time, however, Andrew and I were able to breathe a giant sigh of relief when we were told we were expecting a healthy baby girl. The original measurements had been off due to her positioning at the last visit.

Over the next few months, I was determined to enjoy this pregnancy. There had been so much sadness and fear and uncertainty when I was carrying Isaac that the celebration of carrying a life inside me was muted by such heavy things. It started out with finding a name worthy of Isaac's soon-to-be little sister. This time around, there was no question what middle name we would use. Hope was always going to be a part of her birth story too. Yet her bigger story was my dream of a name that I had always held close since visiting Italy and falling in love with a beautiful town called Siena.

During my time there, not only was I captivated by the famous orange hue that fell over the city at sunset but by its rich history and culture. On a tour we took through the *contradas*, I learned that each of these seventeen neighborhoods had its own little community within the town. On a city level, the contradas had a more competitive angle as they provided a horse from each area in their annual version of the Kentucky Derby. The thing that I was so drawn to though was a sociologic research study done on how Siena had so little crime compared to most European cities. The theory goes that because of the way families have an open-door policy within their contradas, the neighbors essentially serve as an extension of one another, allowing for a much safer childhood for kids—proving that it really does take a village to raise a child.

With this name in mind, our Siena Hope was prayed over at my baby shower that she too would grow up with this community of support. The same group of prayer warriors that rallied behind Isaac believed in her miracle of life just as much. It was so important for me from day one to have some normalcy to this pregnancy, like baby registries and showers and getting the nursery set up. Beyond that, I wanted Siena to know that she wasn't coming into this world under her big brother's shadow. There is a term for children born after the loss of a child or pregnancy, a rainbow baby. Often, this next child comes with bittersweet parental emotions as you mourn one and celebrate the next. But I have also heard of such incredible stories of healing and grace that come out of it too. For me, Siena was that.

Since we had done such an incredible beach photo shoot when I was pregnant with Isaac, I wanted to do something more intimate with our family of three going on four. I had a vision of capturing the silhouette of me holding Isaac and Andrew kissing my belly, suggesting we were recognizing that we weren't fully complete until Siena came along to even us out. I also treated myself to a painted belly cast as a memory of carrying such a special gift. She was due right around Easter, and the irony of it being the same week we had received Isaac's diagnosis just two years prior wasn't lost on me. God was giving me yet another reminder of His constant promise to carry us through with this perfectly healthy baby girl I was expecting.

Siena Hope was born on Tuesday, March 24. Everything about her birth felt strong and a proclamation of health and healing. I got the gift of skin-to-skin time shortly after I came out of the recovery room. The nurses brought her into my private room, and I admired her pink lips that looked just like mine. She latched right away and slept well. She wanted to nurse around the clock, but I didn't mind. I was reveling in having my newborn with me just an hour after she was born. After the typical post-birth hospital dinner with steak and a bottle of sparkling cider, my parents brought Isaac in to meet his baby sister. I had wanted my family to be here for Siena's birth as I had wanted to make sure that my mom and I could bring in this daughter together. The moment she came in and saw me holding her newest grandbaby, the tears flowed freely, with sighs of thankful praise in welcoming Siena to our family.

Andrew walked Isaac over to the bed and placed him next to me. Siena was sleeping on a floral nursing pillow on my lap when big brother leaned over to admire her. At just nineteen months old, he seemed to recognize that she was his baby, and he giggled with glee. I passed Siena to my mom so I could properly get in a hug for Isaac to let him know that he was still my number one guy. As I watched my mom holding her granddaughter for the first time, my heart was bursting with happiness that she would get to watch me raise my own sweet girl. What an incredibly powerful moment it was. We were discharged the next day.

Adjusting to life with two kids under two years old and just nineteen months apart was pretty shocking. Isaac wasn't sleeping through the night or walking unassisted yet. Andrew and I quickly adopted the man-to-man child coverage at bedtime, and I relied heavily on a double stroller to accomplish anything outside of the house. Aside from the typical sleepless nights and trying to figure out our new normal, it was a fairly smooth transition.

Isaac continued to get home visits from Edmarc and have a handful of therapists visit each month. These frequent visitors were a great support to what often felt like a secluded new-mom life. Thankfully, this time around, I had well-established weekly friend playdates with our friends Marisa and her son, Beau, as well as with another best friend from church, Christy, and her daughter, Elliotte. Because we were smack in the middle of the rainy spring East-Coast weather, I dreaded packing the kids in the car for anything. Most of our adventures out were dual purpose; for example, using trips to the doctors in Portsmouth as an excuse to go to Christy's house just around the block. I timed our mornings at the library around when I would be picking up groceries in their pre-order drive-up. Through it all, I was constantly reminded of the calm that came from having a healthy baby and no extra worries on top of simply caring for my newborn.

That summer was filled with all the usual things: trips to the botanical gardens to play in the splash pad, visiting the aquarium, going to our favorite library and, on occasion, braving the beachfront. We packed in the memories of what would be our last East-Coast summer and Isaac's last weeks before he started school. In August, we had an epic train birthday party with an incredible cake made for us by a program called Icing Smiles. I made a Pinterest-inspired cardboard cutout of Thomas the Train for the kids to stick their faces in to pose as the conductor. I even braved a full-scale graham-cracker train activity in which the kids got to decorate their creations with chocolate-covered pretzel steering wheels, licorice train tracks, and Oreo train wheels, along with animal crackers and lumber pretzel sticks to transport. Our sweet boy "choo choo'ed into two" with flare. It was particularly fun to have many of his therapists and the friends we had met through Edmarc stop in to celebrate with us.

Virginia offers early intervention through each school district, starting at age two. Isaac was able to take advantage of this program, and our big boy took the bus off to nursery school in September. On his first day of school, we sat on our front porch stoop, with Isaac's transportation backpack next to him. When the yellow bus pulled up, his eyes got wide with excitement. I carried him up the stairs and strapped him into his safety buckles in the front seat next to the driver. He thought it was the best thing ever. I couldn't believe that my two-year-old was going off to school without me on a bus with total strangers, and he didn't even cry. To this day, I think he would still prefer to take the bus rather than have me drive him to school!

These few hours while Isaac was at school allowed time for me to have one-on-one "girl mornings" with Siena and to enjoy getting to know her blossoming personality. She was flying through her milestones from day one and was always interested in seeing what her big brother was up to. It felt nice to slow down in time and have a few hours of just us before Isaac came home from school. It also allowed me to get in coffee dates with my best friends and bask in the wonder of how different motherhood felt this second go-round. Siena was a good baby. She traveled well with me, and I could take her pretty much anywhere in her carrier. I didn't have to worry if we would be home for her naptime because she slept peacefully no matter where we were. The biggest difference was being able to breastfeed her on demand, something Isaac always had difficulty with. The stress of having to pump and warm a bottle wasn't an issue this time around, and it made life so much easier.

Chapter 14

*Trust in the Lord with all your heart and lean not on
your own understanding; in all your ways acknowledge
him, and he will make your paths straight.*
—Proverbs 3:5–6

I don't remember the specifics of when Andrew and I first started discussing whether he would get out of the Navy at the end of his six-year contract. I do remember weighing heavily the pros and cons of our choices. On the one hand, free military health insurance couldn't be beat. To this day, there is no telling what the future of Isaac's medical needs will be. To have an exceptional team all in one place was probably the number one benefit we got from our military experience. On the other hand, living on the opposite seaboard from our families and dealing with the uncertainties of deployment were tough contenders for finding our way back into the civilian world. While our community of friends in the Hampton Roads area was by far the best support we had ever experienced, many of them were just as likely as us to be facing sea rotations or new orders to other commands. In the end, Andrew and I decided that this was the season for family first.

All through October, we scheduled final playdates, dinners, and doctors' appointments as we prepared to say goodbye to our life in Virginia. I was particularly sentimental thinking about leaving the place where our children had been born. The friendships we had made in Virginia Beach were deeply rooted in military and church family. These people had celebrated with us in our highest of highs and been on their knees praying alongside us at our darkest lows.

There was no replacing people who just showed up when there were no words left to say and when there was nothing they could do to fix an impossible situation. As we learned with our experience with Edmarc Children's Hospice, having a healthy discharge doesn't mean the end of a relationship. It is an opportunity to support each other in a new season of life.

The last week before we moved, our best friends, Marisa and Andy, held a going-away party for us. We shared great food, lots of laughter, and even more photos to document our time together. Their small military-housing living room was packed to the brim with all of our favorite people. I couldn't help but smile as I watched all the toddlers on the floor playing, happy and content together. It was bittersweet having to say goodbye to such amazing friends. The next night, I took the kids to the Edmarc Fall Festival, and we made the rounds about the room, giving hugs and tears freely to the beautiful nurses, social workers, and other hospice staff who had been such a meaningful part of our family journey. Then on Halloween, Andrew drove the kids and me to the airport with three big suitcases, two diaper bags, two car seats, a stroller, and our cat as he sent us on ahead to California. As I kissed him goodbye at Norfolk International, I prayed that he would find his own closure and get to say his farewells from this challenging six years in the Navy.

As Andrew finished up his last month of his military commitments on the East Coast, the kids and I were moving into our rental home back in California, with the help of my parents and in-laws. I had flown out two months previously to attend a week of on-the-job training and sign my official paperwork for an alternative education counseling position with the Yolo County Office of Education. The trip served a dual purpose, allowing me to tour a few rental houses and trying to find a landing place for us in the midst of such a big transition. It also gave me a chance to scope out the kids' daycare center that they would be attending when I went back to work full-time. As I drove our rental car down to the end of the street, where our little green-and-brick rental sat in a lovely, well-established cul-de-sac, I knew that we had found a place we could call home for a while. The giant backyard was reason enough that the kids would love living there. The two-car detached garage behind our fenced property line allowed for easy storage and access to the kids' outdoor toys and gave Andrew a place in the driveway for his firepit. I loved the kids' corridor in the front of the house where they had their own separate bedrooms and bath in a hallway that could be closed off during naptimes. In one short weekend, we unpacked the bare bones of our luggage and finalized arrangements for my first day of work and the kids' start of day care.

That November is still a total blur of my sleeping on a futon with the kids in pack-and-plays and our live-in nanny, Hannah, on a blow-up mattress in the guest room. I was not prepared to be working full-time and leaving my nine-month-old and two-and-a-half-year-old at day care from eight to five. I was not prepared for solo parenting two kids under three. I was also not prepared for moving back home and feeling totally out of place in the town where I had lived for the greater majority of my life. Luckily, I was also not prepared for the outpouring of love and support that my village of family and friends would show in coming together to help in this big transition home. Our rental house was just a few blocks away from my parents and less than a mile from the family I had grown up nannying. Their eldest daughter, Aunty Han, was just twenty-one at the time but graciously offered to help me manage nights with the kids and slept in Isaac's room as he adjusted to the new space. Her youngest sister, Abbey, was in sixth grade and would come over after school and on weekends to serve as big sister to my kids and mother's helper to me. Their mom, Kate, one of my closest friends and confidants before I got married, was always available for us to stop by if we needed a change of scenery and adult conversation.

Our first POD with our belongings arrived two weeks after we did, and a little sense of normalcy crept in as I arranged familiar comfort items around the house. It was a much more welcoming space to have the kids' rooms decorated and a few of their favorite toys and activity stations set up in the living room by the beautiful brick fireplace. I particularly enjoyed having my fully stocked and organized kitchen in place after eating macaroni and cheese off of paper plates those early weeks. My new job as an alternative education counselor for the County Office of Education felt like the perfect fit. The kids were adjusting to day care with far fewer challenging goodbyes than I had expected. And weekly dinners and get-togethers with my parents, Nana and Papa, became a new tradition. The last week of November, Andrew turned in the keys to our military base housing in Virginia and hopped in his Jeep to make the final physical and emotional move out of the Navy. We celebrated a late Thanksgiving with our parents and siblings and truly felt thankful in our opportunity to all be together again.

Once Andrew was home, the kids didn't hesitate to show us that they were going to make memories in this new place. Siena started crawling within the first few weeks, and by December, both children had taken their first steps. If ever there was a milestone that made me stop and want to shout from the rooftops in celebration of our miracle Isaac, it was watching him walk unassisted in our backyard. We had been practicing walking with him, holding a single hand, almost everywhere we went. But as soon as Andrew or I let go, Isaac would always drop slowly to his knees and crawl. This particular afternoon, we were in our backyard exploring the garden beds, while Siena sat bundled in her pink Sherpa snowsuit. I was standing with Isaac by the back door, and he started to walk me over to see Sister. I let go of his hand, and this time, he didn't hesitate to keep going. I pulled out my phone in disbelief as he proceeded to take close to forty steps until he sat down next to Siena on the flannel-lined sleeping bag we had laid out on the grass. Through tears of joy, my heart found confirmation that this was a new season for us, a season of growing and overcoming.

Isaac's services came together through a local program called Alta Regional Center, where he quickly got back into receiving home therapy. Grandma Julie was able to pick him up early from day care some days to have physical and occupational therapy at our house. His feeding and infant therapist typically visited him at day care during lunch or free play to help with self-care habits. With my inside knowledge at the County Office of Education, we got on the calendar for his preschool assessment as well. Also, while health insurance proved to be more expensive than we had prepared for, referrals to the top-rated neurologist and neurosurgeons at UC Davis Medical Center made it feel worthwhile.

We also found that the transition home to the church where Andrew and I had met in junior high brought a built-in community of people who had been praying over our family the previous few years. Andrew's childhood best friend and best man in our wedding had just taken on the job as youth pastor for First Baptist Church of Davis. We were happy to come alongside him and support his ministry. Our once common fears of dropping off Isaac at a new church nursery weren't there in this place where we knew so many people and could figure out navigating inclusion. Their two-to-one ratio of volunteers and their acceptance of having Isaac in the nursery alongside of Siena were a blessing to us.

This was also a lucky thing we stumbled on in our Christian day-care providers: a nursery school that could accommodate both a baby and a toddler with medical needs. Isaac was able to transition through the age groups at his own pace, which often led to him getting to stay with Siena during the day and go through various milestones side-by-side. A huge benefit of this time was the swap of Andrew going back to school while I worked full-time. His taking online classes gave him the flexibility to get the kids to and from day care as necessary and provided a back-up plan if they were sick and needed to stay home. It was a hard season for both of us as we wished we could reverse roles, but I am so proud of us for the way we were able to support each other through the challenges it brought.

The abrupt shift in my going back to work full-time led to a change in our parenting balance and the family routine we had been accustomed to with the Navy. Andrew is very project-based and thrives with having seen the accomplishments of his workday. While going back to school provided some of this structure for him, the challenges of multiple breaks in his day to get the kids to and from day care felt like an interruption in his productivity. I, on the other hand, enjoyed the satisfaction of working with the tough teenagers in the juvenile justice system but felt drained by the weekend when I wanted to be dedicating my time to adventures with my own young children. I also saw the void of playdates and spending time making connections with new mom friends that were hindered by my lack of availability during the week.

One of the hardest things I experienced those first months of moving home was the loss of my beloved grandmother. My mom's mom, Grandma Mary, passed away that December, just a week before I had plans to take the kids down to meet her for the first time. I had wanted to visit her over Thanksgiving break, but the kids had been sick, and it didn't work out. I don't regret many things in life, but the missed opportunity to get a four-generation picture with Grandma, my mom, me, and the kids is something I think about every Christmas.

Grandma Mary was the strongest woman I ever met. I was her eldest grandchild, one of three, and we had an extremely strong connection. She lived about an hour away from us in Martinez, where my mom was born and raised. My grandfather, John Baldwin, was a California congressman until his early death from cancer in 1966. My grandma was fifty, and my mom, the youngest of three daughters, was only eleven. Grandma never remarried and spent the next few years as a stay-at-home mom. Her eldest daughter, my aunt Georgia, was born severely autistic. I like to think that my interest in adaptive aquatics was inspired by her. My fondest memories of Georgia were watching her play at the beach. She loved the water, and although she was nonverbal, you could see the excitement in her eyes when she swam. When Georgia began to need additional help with self-care and education, she moved into a group home for children with disabilities. Georgia passed in her mid-forties, another family member lost to cancer too soon.

Every holiday I can remember from growing up includes standout memories at Grandma Mary's house. Family was something she held dear, and she passed down that love of tradition to my mom and Aunt Doris. Even as an only child with just two cousins on my mom's side, I always spent holidays with extended family at Grandma's house. Easter was a particularly big event as Grandma's early April birthday often fell close to that holiday. I remember the house being filled to the brim with great-aunts and second cousins, along with the immediate family members.

Thanksgiving was a close second in major holiday get-togethers. My grandfather's ancestry could be traced back to the Mayflower, and I can't tell you how many times I was reminded of being the littlest pilgrim growing up! But Christmas was always my favorite. There was something special about being given the reins to decorate Grandma's tree as a little girl. I remember her delicate blown-glass ornaments and the vintage white Santa's sleigh I got to put up on the mantle.

When I was little, these were the things I held dear about Grandma's house. When I got into high school, my understanding of what an incredible woman she was began to grow. For one, she was the most generous person I had ever known. My grandfather's family had owned a ranch in Danville, and when he died, she sold the land. You would never have known she had any wealth. She lived a contented middle-class life on a day-to-day basis and was well-known in the community for her involvement in various women's groups and charities. Her love of travel and spirit of adventure set her apart from the rest, though.

I like to think that I inherited as much from my grandmother as I did from my mom. There was a certain level of strength and independence that I admired about both of them. My grandmother certainly had a tough hand dealt to her with the early death of my grandfather and raising her three girls alone, not to mention the challenges she must have faced raising a daughter with autism in a generation that had little information about the diagnosis. Both she and my mom valued the role of motherhood in a way that gave their children a stable household and yet equal opportunity to be involved with things to grow into and dream about.

Education held a lot of weight in my family. I looked at colleges as early as seventh grade. But it was my grandma who financed both my undergrad and master's programs and gave me the chance to pursue those early career plans. When it came time to write my master's thesis, I took my love of all things to do with physical education and found a way to tie it into my budding passion for counseling. Ultimately, I wrote an adaptive physical aquatics program guide for my hometown. I credited my grandma and my aunt Georgia for giving me a unique perspective on families of children with special needs and the opportunities that aren't always available to them.

Over the years, I sought out ways to be involved in special-needs sports programs, where my drive to open doors to everyone and provide equal access kept me going. When I found out I was pregnant with a child who would likely have severe disabilities if born alive, Grandma was the only person I really knew who had been through something similar to me. Sadly, by that time, she had significant memory loss from old age. I never got to ask her about raising a child with special needs, but when it came time to name our firstborn, I made sure to give a nod to Grandma. While we primarily chose the name Isaac from the Bible, it also was a way for me to carry a piece of Grandma's heritage as her maiden name was Isaacs.

In the thirty-three years I had with Grandma Mary, considerably my closest relative, we still only saw each other consistently at holidays and on birthdays. We did have some epic vacations together, including a time in Europe when I kept her from being robbed by a purse snatcher. But we never had the privilege of afterschool playdates or her attending any of my sports events. It meant a lot to me when we moved home from Virginia and were able to give our kids the chance to see both sets of grandparents on a weekly basis.

The biggest thing that stands out to me about that first year at home was the time with family. Beyond my working full-time and Andrew being in school full-time, there wasn't a lot of opportunity to have much going on. With medical history like ours, this year also felt uneventful because of the newfound stability in health we were blessed with. While we did go through two terrible rounds of hand-foot-and-mouth disease, we were thankful for the bigger picture of no seizures or surgeries.

I was so disappointed that we had to postpone Siena's first birthday celebration three times due to the wretched hand-foot-and-mouth. But when we finally got around to celebrating, it was perfect. I looked at my backyard full of loved ones all chatting merrily while sitting on picnic blankets and watching the kids play. That moment in time was exactly what I had imagined for my kids growing up. Even more beautifully full circle was our first Easter at my parents' house and the chance to start new memories and traditions there in Grandma Mary's honor.

That summer, I also got to enjoy some stay-at-home mommy moments as my school-based job had me on a two-hundred-day yearly contract. I had six incredible weeks of vacation, the kids had a month-and-a-half without any day care, and Andrew rounded out our time off to give all four of us time together at home. The kids and I got to take part in our first of many downtown Fourth-of-July bike parades. Then Andrew and I escaped to Lake Tahoe for a long weekend with Siena, while Isaac hung out with the grandparents. Our family of four went to the state fair to indulge Isaac's continued interest in all things farm. And we bravely ventured off the grid to our church's family camp at Pilot Lake. It was a much-needed break for all of us to enjoy the long California days and introduce the kids to all of our favorite summer spots.

Isaac celebrated his third birthday a week before school started, and then we were back up and running at full speed. The preschool program he attended matched him with a one-on-one aide in a least-restrictive, special-education classroom. Isaac started with half days and split his afternoons between grandparents. My job still felt like the right place to be at and awarded me the chance to have a similar school schedule and holidays. Isaac's aide, Miss Alyssa, became our nanny, and Andrew and I enjoyed having someone familiar with special needs available for us to use on date nights.

I tried to maximize my time with the kids on weekends, especially Siena, as I had major mommy guilt for her having to be in day care full-time. Most weekends, we went to the zoo and its neighboring Fairytale Town in Sacramento. When we weren't there, I made a valiant effort to scout out local neighborhood parks that Isaac could navigate easily. We basked in the California weather as summer's dry heat slowly turned into beautiful autumn days. Before we knew it, the next round of holidays were upon us, and we were enjoying the task of having to figure out how to see everyone on both sides of the family to celebrate.

With Andrew's official one-year Navy veteran anniversary under his belt in January, we finally started to feel like we were matriculating back into civilian life. So much so that in February, we moved out of our rental house with the big backyard and into one we could call our very own about a mile away. Tucked away in another cul-de-sac, our little blue house was the perfect starter home for our family of four to grow up in. With the large living room and vaulted ceilings, we were able to create a play area in one half of the room and the sitting area and TV on the other side of the brick fireplace. The kitchen stove gave me a direct view to be able to watch the kids while I was busy making dinner. It was move-in ready, with barely any home renovation projects needed. We were less than five minutes away from my work, my parents, and the elementary school Isaac would later attend. For peace of mind, the nearest hospital was also just three blocks away.

Most of the free time in the following months was spent settling into our forever home. I painted our kitchen cabinets with chalk paint over my spring break, and Andrew tackled our backyard over his. For Siena's second birthday, we hosted our first family gathering and had a great sense of accomplishment and belonging in the process.

Chapter 15

*Come to me, all you who are weary and burdened, and I will
give you rest. Take my yoke upon you and learn from me, for
I am gentle and humble in heart, and you will find rest for
your souls. For my yoke is easy and my burden is light.*
—Matthew 11:28–30

Unfortunately, as is common in life, when one area is thriving,
another seems to struggle. That spring, two back-to-back incidents
at work left me feeling like my safety was at risk on the job. Having
worked in alternative education for close to four years at that point, I
had always felt like the reward of serving at-risk youth in the juvenile
justice system outweighed the concerns. Yet the things that happened
in a period of less than ten days shook me to my core, and my mental
health began to backslide.

Every time I previously felt like there was stability in my life, I
would question whether I should wean myself off my anxiety medication. But in the blink of an eye, some major event would throw my
mind back into swirling chaos. It felt like a revolving door that I was
trapped in. Looking out of it, everything appeared bright and shiny
and felt warm and new. As soon as I tried to get out, I would face the
cold wind, the fast-paced noises of life, and the brutal loneliness of
nameless faces on the street.

Thankfully, over the years, I had good doctors, counseling
resources, and a focus on health and wellness that allowed me to find a
good balance of stability with my anxiety. When things started falling
apart after the big events at work, I knew that it was time for a change,
not just for me but so that my family could have the best me too.

Ironically, that April, I had an opportunity to share my testimony about Isaac's birth story at our church's spring ladies' retreat. I love to look back and see God's hand in things, and this certainly provided me with the stage I needed to tell my story, feel heard, and be seen. It opened doors to new friendships at church and new relationships with other families with young kids. I began to see how isolated I had been in the community sense since moving home.

In Virginia, without any family close by, our church friends filled every space of our relational circle. They were temporary sisters and brothers, aunts and uncles, moms and dads, and every relationship I needed. They were my East Coast family. Thankfully, family is a bond for life, and the people who meant the most to me in Virginia have kept in touch ever since. That summer, for an early birthday present, I flew cross-country with Siena for a week-long stay at Christy's house and a chance to catch up with my best girlfriends. It was the respite I needed to get some clarity in my mind and some courage in my heart to reach out and get more involved at home to build new relationships there.

It was a good thing too because that fall, Andrew started a new business program at school that had all night classes. Isaac had just turned four, and Siena was two-and-a-half, so dinner and bedtimes took all my strength every night. It felt like a new season and a new challenge of parenting. We have experienced the full gamut of things in the attempt to balance our married life that go beyond being a Navy spouse and special-needs parent—the give-and-take of who is working full-time or staying home full-time versus being a full-time student or unemployed. If my anxiety is a revolving door, our life situations are like a box of Bertie Botts Every Flavor Beans. These jelly beans, made famous in the Harry Potter book series by J. K. Rowling, vary from the typical delicious candy flavors to the complete odd and disgusting, like earwax and booger flavored.

Any given month at our house, you could reach into the proverbial candy bag and pick out a colorful bean, never knowing whether it would be a tasty treat of good news or a gut-wrenching challenge you just want to spit out immediately and say "Next!" What was especially hard during that particular season of life was not feeling like I could talk about what was happening in the way that I normally do. By nature, I loathe meaningless chitchat and desire more than anything to have depth in relationships. Confined by the time constraints of working full-time and taking care of two kids, I didn't have as much chance to take advantage of the fledgling friendships I was developing with ladies from church. My usual need for in-person processing became more of a desire for blogging. It is such a fine line to be true to one's story and also protect the people who are a part of it.

Soon enough, we had news worth sharing with everyone. Isaac's neurologist had decided that two years seizure-free was the mark he had been waiting for to start weaning him off of his medicine. At the time, Isaac was taking a weight-based dose of a liquid med and a pill med two times daily. Between Thanksgiving and Christmas break, we started to cut back on the pill dose. When Isaac returned to school in January, it was like his teachers were meeting a brand-new kid in the classroom.

One of the many downsides to making critical life decisions for your child in a moment of crisis is that, often, you don't have time to do all the research. This sounds terrible, but it rang true for us on more than one occasion. When Isaac started having his uncontrolled breakthrough seizures, we had little choice but to trust the experts to practice best care. Yes, we did go on to research and get second opinions and all that, but the list of pros typically outweigh the cons for such medications. This was definitely true for this pill that Isaac had been taking. But I don't ever remember the doctors explaining the depth of cognitive fog the medicine could induce.

A huge wave of mommy guilt and hindsight is 20/20. I regretted having missed out on all Isaac might have been communicating with us the last two years. It was like the time I went to Costa Rica during grad school to study Spanish and learn about the issues their social workers faced. I left in January with four years of high school and college conversational Spanish and came home in February having spoken zero English the entire time I was away. The fluency change we saw in Isaac was monumental.

When family came to celebrate Siena's third birthday in March, people were teary-eyed listening to Isaac wow the room with his stories and jokes. It felt like milestones were a weekly checklist at that point. Not only were his academics changing, but we saw the strength in his physical abilities coming out as well. One of our favorite things to watch was both kids learning to peddle their tricycles on their own. This rite of passage felt like such a huge celebration as his annual diagnosis day anniversary passed. I wondered how his team of doctors from birth and the group of specialists we had left Virginia with at two would react to seeing Isaac now. Talk about overcoming!

Things were falling into place in many aspects after Isaac stopped the secondary medication. The doctor gave us permission to start weaning him off of the baseline meds at a very slow weekly rate, and that was going well. I had since transferred jobs from the Yolo County Office of Education to the local school district. I took a job as a roving elementary school counselor and split my time between three sites. This position allowed me to have a shorter workday and gave me the chance to take a step away from all the extra duties that come with a managerial job. I also dropped down to a 186-day contract, so my schedule aligned almost exactly with Isaac's school year. Andrew, too, found his groove in the business program and started focusing on getting his accounting degree.

I made a point to research and pursue more opportunities to be involved at church with my modified work schedule. This led to my attending a women's retreat in the Santa Cruz mountains. After that event, I made an effort to keep in touch with church friends during the week and get the kids together for playdates on the weekend. The change in my heart with these new support systems getting stabilized made all the difference.

It was a good thing too because, before we knew it, Isaac was in his final week of weaning off his last seizure medicine. I was so nervous about how things would go once he took his final dose. The happy tears I cried in the moment Isaac took those 0.5 milliliters of his medicine for the last time were short-lived. Within thirty-six hours, he had back-to-back seizures, and the doctor put him back on a low dose. We were nervous wrecks sending him to school and wondering if that was enough. Again, we were put in a place of having to trust the doctor to do the right thing for our kid. Thankfully, Isaac's one-on-one aide, Miss Alyssa, continued to be written into his IEP as a safety measure for him through the years. This was particularly a nice peace of mind when Isaac graduated from his second year of preschool and started summer school at his kindergarten school site.

Our neurologist recommended we get an updated MRI on Isaac since he was overdue for his annual appointment. Typically, the neurosurgeon is the one who orders these, and it got me thinking that it was odd that we hadn't received our yearly call to schedule our checkup. This led to the realization that we had been dropped from our neurosurgeon at UC Davis. Somehow, our insurance providers failed to notify us that they no longer had a contract with them due to rising costs. We quickly got a referral to the next closest pediatric specialist, which turned out to be in San Francisco.

I would go anywhere for my kid to get the care he needs. But the thought of driving to San Francisco, an hour-and-a-half away with no traffic, was a new sort of stress. I was concerned that if we established care at the children's hospital there, and in the event of an emergency, Isaac would likely have to be airlifted to get there in a timely matter. I couldn't imagine that they would transfer him by ambulance if his shunt was failing. I also couldn't imagine having to drive back and forth from the hospital should the time come when he was ever admitted.

I reluctantly went to the appointment anyway since our options for pediatric neurosurgeons were slim. Incredibly, the head of the department was the surgeon assigned to us. As such, the meeting was quick and straight to the point. We would get an MRI, and then we would come back for his opinion. Well that was great, except it was 4:30 p.m. on a Friday, and the call to get approval from our health insurance went straight to voice mail. Miraculously, they called back while I was still at the office, but they said UCSF was technically out-of-area, so it wasn't covered. I was so confused. I didn't know how we got a referral out of our district but then couldn't get the procedure covered. I would be baffled by this lesson numerous times over the next year as I fought to get things done in-house.

I paid for dinner in the hospital café, then paid my ticket for garage parking and then for the toll bridge. Then I sat in Bay area traffic going into the weekend with a bad attitude. On Monday, I went into our pediatrician's office and told our referral lady that we were back at square one. She worked her typical magic, and by week's end, we had an MRI referral to a local hospital in Sacramento.

I took Isaac in bright and early for our appointment, something I am always thankful for since he couldn't eat in the morning before anesthesia. It was also a good thing because I went to the wrong MRI office. It was not a great start, but we still arrived on time for check-in. I was particularly anxious that day because in the calls leading up to the MRI, I had yet to speak with the doctors about Isaac's history with anesthesia. When we met with the nurse for vitals in the hospital room, I asked when I would get to speak with the doctor. She assured me the doctor would be coming in soon.

The next person I saw, however, was not the doctor but the anesthesiologist. We chatted about Isaac's various needs going under and some of the challenges he would have coming out. I asked if the neurosurgeon would be in next, and the anesthesiologist said he would ask. The nurse came back in and said they didn't have a doctor on site because the MRI didn't have any special requests listed. I started to panic and asked how they planned to do Isaac's shunt adjustment without a neurosurgeon. "What shunt adjustment?" they asked.

At this point, the technician had arrived to wheel Isaac back to the procedure room. I literally got up and stood at the curtain, blocking the staff from his hospital bed. I told them that there would be no MRI today, that Isaac needed special shunt equipment and a neurosurgeon in order to have the procedure, neither of which they had available, and none of which anyone had thought to follow up on despite my repeated requests.

I drove Isaac through Chick-fil-A for lunch that afternoon and swore I would never again go to that hospital. I also promised myself that no matter what medical staff told me about standard procedures, Isaac would not be subjected to anything that would jeopardize his health care. I didn't know it at the time, but this was the beginning of my journey as my son's medical social worker.

Chapter 16

God is our refuge and strength, an ever-present help in trouble.
Therefore we will not fear, though the earth give way and the
mountains fall into the heart of the sea, though its waters roar
and foam and the mountains quake with their surging.
                                        —Psalm 46:1–3

The Fourth of July kicked off the beginning of summer vacation, and we attended our small town's annual bike parade downtown. We arrived in time to decorate the kids' bikes in patriotic colors and got in line behind the guests of honor. That year, a local organization for special-needs children, NorCal Trykers, was leading the way. I was familiar with the program for their work with the County Office of Education and the exceptional-needs school they worked with. When we got home that day, I was inspired to look for the bike the next size up for Isaac's birthday since he was outgrowing his first tricycle by then.

One thing led to another, and I eventually got in touch with the director at NorCal Trykers to ask if she had a recommendation for where we could get a modified high-back seat for a larger bicycle. I explained that Isaac's balance was an issue from his various brain conditions and that he was afraid to even get on a bike with training wheels because it lacked back support. Instead of giving me the name of a website or a local bike shop, she said that fate must have brought me to call her. She went on to tell me how the Fourth of July parade had brought in many donations to their charity, but they had few applicants to match bikes with. The next thing I knew, we were scheduling a fitting for Isaac to get one of his very own special-needs tricycles!

One of the beautiful things about the special-needs community is the sharing of resources. When NorCal Trykers arranged for Isaac to get his own bike, they asked where he attended school and if we'd like a bike donated to his class. Not only did they donate Isaac's bike and a classroom bike, but other students were able to get fitted for their own as well. A happy accident of stumbling onto this amazing organization ended in a lot of happy kids receiving a well-deserved gift.

That fall, Isaac started kindergarten, and I went back to work as an elementary school counselor. Siena kept her regular nursery school schedule, and Andrew was in his final semester of his accounting program. Life in our little household seemed to be holding steady. I started attending a twice-monthly women's night at church that provided the social outlet I needed to survive Andrew's four evenings of night school each week. On Saturday, I took the kids to the zoo, Fairytale Town, the aquarium, and children's museum to get out of the house and give Andrew space to study. Sundays, we had family time at church in the morning, with football and laundry in the afternoon and evening. Things were busy, but we seemed to be managing well.

In December, we celebrated Andrew's graduation from his accounting program. We took a collective sigh of relief to have that season behind us and then wondered what in the world would happen next. As a Navy veteran, Andrew had great success working with the local schools' academic vet programs. He was diligent in his research and took all the opportunities available to put himself out there for internships and career days. There were a couple different directions his post-graduation route could go. In the meantime, he was applying for state and federal jobs on a weekly basis.

Just as we had thought we'd had our routine down during fall semester, suddenly, it felt like the bottom had dropped out from under us. How did we expect this to go? That a job would just miraculously be ready on New Year's Day? What happened to all those internship options that we thought were a sure thing? Ultimately, our time line and expectations did not match reality. It is funny how often we panic when things don't turn out at that moment we think they should and how much we don't trust God's timing and the plans He has laid out for us.

Andrew essentially got two job offers at the same time—one at the state level, the other, federal. It became a waiting game of who would get their ducks in a row quickest to have him sign on the dotted line. The timing thing also became clear to us when my declining health brought about the need for surgery. Long story short, despite two pregnancies, my endometriosis was more troubling than ever, and trying to find new treatment options was proving difficult.

Over the holidays, I had started a new medication that triggered my first bout with depression. I did not handle it well. I struggled to get out of bed most days and had more panic attacks than ever before. My overwhelming anxiety completely got in the way of my attendance and job performance at work. It was bad. My gynecologist and I went back to the drawing board and talked about Band-Aid versus bold options. All I knew was that I did not want to live with this debilitating depression. This is how I came to decide on a voluntary hysterectomy at the age of thirty-six.

Andrew's job commitments that spring consisted mainly of paperwork, forms, background checks, and all the things that require you to hurry up and wait. My surgery was scheduled for April so that Andrew would be home with me for the first two essential weeks of post-op recovery. While I tried my best to take care of my physical and mental health, it became clear that Isaac was also struggling. He seemed overly emotional and extra sensitive about things that quickly became worrisome.

After our issues with health insurance the previous summer, Andrew and I decided to wait until open enrollment to change health care providers in order to set up Isaac's MRI. Close to six months had now passed since he should have had the procedure. We got reestablished with UC Davis Neurosurgery after another battle with the referral system and finally had our intake appointment scheduled for Valentine's Day. When I told the doctor my concerns about Isaac, she ordered an MRI stat and agreed it sounded like the possible beginning of shunt failure.

Despite everything we'd done to make the process smooth this time around, we ran into similar issues after the first referral was made to the Sacramento hospital I refused to go back to. UC Davis, for their part, tried to vouch for the need to have Isaac's MRI in-house, but the process took forever. In the meantime, while we waited for the approval we needed, it was time for my surgery.

The hysterectomy itself went well. The doctor was able to save my ovaries so I didn't have to experience surgically induced menopause. Still, it was a long road of recovery of almost a full two months before I was really up and about and back to my normal mommy duties. Our village showed up strong for us during that time when I wasn't allowed to drive or cook or do much for the kids on my own. The grandparents stepped up in a big way, even more than their usual contributions to our family. The kids were well taken care of, and I felt like I had the space to recover on my own time line. My doctor finally cleared me for regular activity in June, just as the kids were getting out for the summer.

Isaac's health needs took over from there, and we scheduled many appointments: medication management and an EEG with his neurologist, CT scan, X-ray and MRI with the neurosurgeon, and a referral to the eye doctor to check the pressure on his occipital nerve. We decided that Isaac would have a shunt adjustment surgery, but the neurosurgeon wanted some other information to determine whether it would be better to do a full replacement. We had always been told that Isaac's shunt from birth had a 50/50 failure rate by the time a child turned seven as there was a lot of stress on the equipment when used in a quickly growing child.

The waiting for each referral and each subsequent appointment and specialist was painstaking. Isaac complained about the sun every time we went out of the house. His balance was funny, and his emotional sensitivity was high. Yet the doctors still said that because he wasn't showing the typical signs of full shunt failure, it was likely just a slow leak or malfunction. Too little too late would we learn that it was a much bigger issue than they had assumed.

Isaac's MRI results came back with clear signs of increased hydrocephalus (swelling of the brain due to excessive cerebral spinal fluid). The eye doctor said his occipital nerve was under severe pressure due to this swelling and referred us to an even bigger, high-profile doctor back at UCSF. Thankfully, Andrew had started his new state job in May, and we had invested in the top-of-the-line health insurance.

It was the first day of school when the pediatric ophthalmology neurologist called me. I had dropped off Isaac with Alyssa at school for the start of first grade. I was shopping for work clothes at the outlet mall about thirty minutes from home. With everything that had happened over the last few months, Andrew and I had decided that I would move to a part-time job since he was in a secure full-time position. My new job wouldn't start for another two weeks, so I was trying to get in a few errands while the kids were back at school.

I was standing in the dressing room about three jeans deep into trying on clothes when I got the call. The high-profile doctor from UCSF called and said that he would not in fact be taking on Isaac's case. Instead, he told me to drop everything and go pick up Isaac from school and take him to the hospital where our neurosurgeon practiced. He explained that Isaac was essentially going blind from the pressure on his optic nerve and that if we didn't do something soon, there would be irreversible damage—not to mention what the fluid build-up was likely doing to his brain. It was the permission I had been waiting for. I left my pile of clothes on the chair and sprinted out of the store like a mad woman. I called Andrew on the way, told him everything, and asked him to meet us at the hospital. I called Siena's preschool and asked if she could stay in after-school care that day until a grandparent could pick her up. I called my in-laws and arranged for Siena to potentially spend a few nights with them. I called my parents, and the tears came.

By the time I arrived at Isaac's school, I tried to put on my bravest face for him. Isaac has always been a feeler. His empathy is off the charts, and he watches the people around him in a way that I've rarely seen a child observe his surroundings. I knew that he would sense that I was worried, and I wanted to be strong for him as

I explained what was happening. For better or worse, throughout all of Isaac's many doctor appointments, he has come to the conclusion that the doctor's office is a safe space where people make him feel better. Even beyond his anxiety and fear when he knows the IV is about to happen, he still recognizes that going to the doctor or hospital in itself isn't scary.

As we waited in the emergency room, I pulled out our hospital go-bag that I had ready. We had barely pulled out the first activity when they called us back for the intake. Isaac was immediately given a private room in the pediatric unit, and the waiting game began. The doctors all affirmed our decision to bypass the insurance's snail-pace approval time line and just make things happen. Despite all the encouragement, we waited eight hours before Isaac was admitted to the PICU. Poor Isaac had multiple blood draws, three failed IV attempts, and a mini version of the shunt test where they did a needle tap. It was no fun for any of us involved. By nine thirty that night, we both fell asleep, exhausted from the events of the day. Even now, reliving those hours, days, and weeks feels like a raw place that I am still trying to wrap my mind around. My heart aches at the trauma that Isaac went through with all the various needles and procedures. There is no describing watching your baby go through brain surgery. But I was not prepared to watch my six-year-old endure it again.

Isaac was admitted to the Pediatric ICU at the UC Davis hospital in Sacramento on Andrew's thirty-fifth birthday; our plans for a dinner date that night forgotten and reservations canceled. I spent the night with Isaac as we waited for a slot in the OR to open up, while Andrew went home to try to explain to Siena what was going on. On Thursday, we woke up to the news that we were bypassing a full shunt study based on the results of the needle tap. We were officially on board for surgery, but still, there was no space in the OR at the time. The waiting game continued, this time with no food or water allowed. Sweet Isaac was a happy camper as he visited the child life playroom and had quiet time with Andrew and me. At 1:30 p.m., we got word that all systems were a go, and Isaac was prepped for surgery. Two hours later, we got the call that told us surgery was a success. The tubing in his brain to the ventricles was the culprit of the hydrocephalus, and the neurosurgeon said the shunt itself was wedged in tight. She replaced the tubing and did a full swap out of his old shunt and replaced it with the newest brand and technology. This shunt still had a magnetic programming option, but this one would be much easier to adjust manually.

Isaac slept most of the afternoon and into the evening, until Grandma and Grandpa brought Siena and Aunt C in for a visit. The doctors reported immediate evidence of the pressure in his eyes lessening. He ended up sleeping through the night with a Tylenol drip and extra meds for breakthrough pain. On Friday morning, he woke up sleepy but back to his happy self. We went to the playroom again as we awaited word on whether or not they would do an MRI before he was discharged. Before we could get on the schedule for imaging, they downgraded us from the PICU to the pediatric floor. After our neurologist came in to visit and update us on the plan, she called back to say that she would postpone the MRI out a week so that the scan wouldn't cause Isaac unneeded stress so soon after surgery. She felt like he looked well enough and was responding to the surgery in a way that made her comfortable with discharging him. We were sent home with strict orders to bring Isaac back to the ER immediately if we had any concerns. Mainly, they were worried about blood clots forming from the removal of the first shunt, so we would need to be mindful of the severity of this possibility. We got exit papers around three that afternoon and made our way home with a follow-up scheduled with neurosurgery for Tuesday.

That weekend, Andrew and I tried our best to keep Isaac in a calm state of recovery. He had a different plan in mind and kept asking us to go outside to ride scooters or play soccer with him. We were thankful that he was feeling so well and wanting to get back into the swing of things, but it is hard to convince a determined six-year-old boy that he needs to stay inside. Luckily, we had a variety of his favorite faces stop by to visit and entertain him with board games and other low-key activities. Alyssa came by with cards from his school mates and a sweet book about what happens when dinosaurs get sick. I took Siena to church at FBC on Sunday morning and was thankful for a brief respite out of the house surrounded by people who'd been praying for us.

Monday morning, Isaac woke up crying, and I could tell something was not right. He had been a little wobbly on his feet over the weekend, but I assumed it was just the shunt adjustments getting settled. The fever he spiked with told me otherwise, and his insistence that his eyes were still hurting told me we should go back into the hospital. I dropped off Siena to school on our way to Sacramento and updated Andrew along the way. We stayed in the ER for eleven hours while we had fresh labs drawn and a new round of imaging. They did a second shunt tap, which was even more horrific than the first time they tried it a few days previously. Essentially, they needed to take a giant needle and stick it into the shunt reservoir to see how much fluid they could remove in order to determine if the flow was correct. The first time they did it bedside in the ER, they gave Isaac some anxiety meds to take the edge off. I told the doctors there was no way he would sit through the procedure fully conscious, but they tried anyway. It did not go well, and this time around, they took me a bit more seriously.

Unfortunately, this meant Isaac was doped up on the heaviest drugs he had ever been given in order to do a partial sedation. I was hesitant to even allow them to do this as they rattled off the potential side effects, but the doctors said that insurance would not permit them to do full anesthesia for the procedure. I signed the permission forms, and the meds were given intravenously. As soon as Isaac saw the number of surgical interns coming into the room with oxygen, he started to get hysterical. I was sitting behind him on his hospital bed in the ER, bear-hugging him as best as I could as the lead intern moved in to take the shunt tap. It took about ten minutes in total, but it felt like ten hours as I sat there with arms clenched and jaw tight, trying to hold it together. Afterward, one of the surgical residents commented on how stoic I was and said I must be made of tougher stuff than them. Everyone left a little bit shaken.

Eventually, we were admitted to the pediatric floor to wait for the results of all the various labs and tests Isaac had done earlier in the day. We spent the night and waited around until late afternoon. The doctors said preliminary bacterial growth was negative for the shunt tap, and all the essential labs came back negative. The team thought that Isaac's body was most likely trying to adjust to the new foreign object that had been placed in it and that we should go home and try to get some rest. I kept Isaac home for the week per post-brain-surgery requirements, and we tried to stay busy without going stir crazy. On Thursday, we had our post-op neurosurgery visit. We found out that the full results of the shunt tap had actually grown into a positive infection after the full seventy-two hours. It was recommended that we go to our queen magician of referrals at our pediatric primary doctor and beg and plead to get anesthesia approved for a full twenty-minute shunt study. We got approval on Friday and were scheduled for the procedure on Monday. I took Siena on a special mother/daughter date with a friend of hers from gymnastics to make sure she was hanging in there amidst all the uncertainty and adjustments. She was by far the biggest trooper of that whole time, and I was amazed at how brave she was for Isaac.

We knew Isaac hadn't been feeling well, and with the positive infection results, Andrew and I were keeping an extra close eye on him. After a few days of lethargy, Isaac started throwing up. We debated whether this was just a stomach bug thing, while I double-checked that our hospital go-bag was refilled with all the necessities. I told Andrew I didn't feel comfortable waiting for our doctor's appointment the following day and packed Isaac in the car. As I was exiting the freeway to the UCD Med Center, I looked back to make sure Isaac still had his sick bag handy if he needed it. I caught a glimpse of his eyes rolling back in his head as he lost consciousness and started to have a seizure. I called 911 and told them that I was mere blocks from the ER and asked if they could have someone waiting for us outside.

I pulled up just outside the entrance, and there were three emergency responders at the front desk waiting to scoop Isaac up from my arms and get him into a bed while I parked. We were led back to an isolated private room due to Isaac's infection and sat in limbo waiting to be admitted to an open room in PICU. Around one in the morning, we finally wheeled Isaac's bed up to the tenth floor. After an uneventful night of sleep, thanks to a good dose of Zofran to ease Isaac's upset tummy, we woke up to the news that our slot in the OR had been bumped up for a higher-level emergency. Back at home, I learned that Siena also had a tummy bug, and I prayed that Andrew and I wouldn't get sick.

By the end of the day, our neurosurgeon came up and said there weren't any signs that we would get into the OR soon, and would it be okay if we did the procedure bedside. I looked at the two residents who had gone through the shunt taps with us in the ER and said that we would have to do something better for Isaac than the failed sedation he had before. The head pediatric anesthesiologist came up and assured me that everything they'd be doing was exactly how they would have done it in the OR, just without the space itself. I felt defeated, wondering if this would go poorly too. Thankfully, I watched Isaac fall asleep before my eyes as the team quickly moved in to do the necessary procedure.

Twenty-four hours later, we learned that Isaac would need to go back in for yet another surgery to fix the catheter of his new shunt, something the neurosurgeon had caught on the most recent imaging. Finally, it seemed like the team had figured out what was wrong, and I was glad they would be taking care of it on this third admission to the hospital since the initial surgery. Andrew took the day off from work, and Siena was in good hands at her grandparents' house. Surgery fixed the necessary wrongs, and Isaac came out of the recovery room and slept most of the day as his brain healed. After four days, we were discharged one last time, and I took Isaac home to have a quiet night before we got Siena.

After the long weekend at home to recover, we got the all-clear to go back to school. Isaac had strict orders to stay close to Miss Alyssa, and he wasn't able to participate in PE or recess yet. He spent the next two weeks doing modified activities in which there wasn't so much risk of him falling or getting hit in the head at random. The MRI was the last hurdle we had to clear, both with health insurance and Isaac's final thumbs-up for healing.

I wove through the familiar maze of empty hallways at the UCD Med Center on my way to take Isaac to the MRI room located in the farthest back corner of the hospital. When we arrived, it was clear that my efforts to prepare the team beforehand had been taken seriously. The child life specialist was paged and came to sit on the floor with Isaac while we waited for his procedure. The VIP treatment continued as we were taken into a corner room and the curtains drawn. The doctors said they would give Isaac time to adjust to an oral medication that would help to sedate him. While we waited the twenty minutes for it to kick in, the child life specialist played Isaac's favorite show, *Blippi*, on the hospital iPad. She chatted easily with him about the silly episode, and soon, we saw his eyes start to droop. The anesthesiologist poked his head around the curtain and handed me an oxygen mask. I put it on Isaac, and the rest of the necessary sedation took him into a calm sleep. They quickly and quietly moved to take him to the MRI room down the hall, and within the hour, I met him upstairs at the third floor recovery room.

Again, the child life specialist was there waiting with us and asking how they could make our experience more comfortable. Isaac took an extra-long time to come off sedation, and I was worried we wouldn't make our 4:45 p.m. appointment at the neurosurgery clinic to have his shunt programmed to the correct setting post MRI. She relayed the message to the nurses' desk, and they paged the on-call resident. As Isaac was coming to, one of our neurosurgery team members from the previous hospital stay showed up and took care of the shunt on the spot. We sat for a while longer and had popsicles while Isaac came around fully. That day driving home from the hospital, I finally was able to see how my voice had been heard and changes had been made to make things better for my son's care.

Conclusion

Grief is like the ocean. It comes in waves ebbing and flowing. Sometimes the water is calm, and sometimes it's overwhelming. All we can do is learn to swim.

—Vicki Harrison

It has been about three months since Isaac was in and out of the hospital for nearly three weeks. It has seemed a natural time of reflection as we just rang in the new year of 2020. A stranger wouldn't know that Isaac had ever gone through what he did so recently, or in his lifetime, for that matter. I have always thought that his joyful personality and zeal for life block out any of the trauma that he has been through. Now more than ever, I am amazed at how he picks right back up where he left off as though he hadn't just come out of brain surgery for the fifth time. Our parent hearts, on the other hand, don't feel quite so sturdy.

Andrew and I have carried around the burden of trauma these last seven years. Some days, we are really good at going through the motions and putting on our happy faces, trying our best to blend in. Other times, when the loose string on the blanket edge begins to unravel, it is all we can do not to watch it spill into a pile of threads on the ground. My counselor brain tries to use the things I have learned and the tools I have gained to cope with the challenges of being a special-needs parent. Still, I often feel so underqualified to be in this position.

When Isaac was in the hospital this fall, I joked with the child life specialists about how I felt that I should add full-time medical family social worker to my résumé. In truth, I use my background as a force to be reckoned with in the fight against health insurance and policy guidelines that don't work for my child's unique case. I take complete advantage of the network of professionals I know through work and community networking. I have dedicated myself to spending the time it takes on the phone or internet to figure out how best to advocate for my family. But again, I come out the other end feeling exhausted.

At a recent holiday gathering with extended family I don't often see, I chatted with someone whose hobby was to run an extreme race in wild country with nothing but a compass. He compared it to Bear Grylls's *Man vs. Wild* TV series, where they drop a previous Marine expert in the middle of nowhere, and he has to fend for himself until he reaches a certain pick-up point. It takes an inordinate amount of training to prepare oneself emotionally and physically for the unexpected challenges that could be faced at any point. Basic needs like safety, shelter, food, and clothing aren't necessarily something that can be relied upon.

Living with trauma feels like this to me. I have done my research on basic parenthood survival. I have talked to experts who have been there before. I have spent time trying to understand the world of special-needs children and what they need to adapt to their surroundings. I have overcome fears about crisis medical situations and conquered my emotional meltdowns when they try to get the best of me. Most days, I really can find the beauty in this journey that I have traveled. Still, there is only so much that can be done to prepare for the natural disasters that come. There is no weather channel app to warn of the impending storm, and no time to prepare other than throwing together what is within reach and doing your best to ride it out. As the storm passes, you pick yourself up and move on toward your destination with whatever resources you have.

For me, the rescue is where it all comes together. I can see the beacon of light revolving on the shoreline, guiding me to safety. I know that the Keeper of this hope and light has stayed awake to show me the way home. The waves may be crashing wildly into the treacherous cliffs, but I find the safest path to shore. Calm waters move to welcome me, and I relax in the comfort of firm ground beneath my feet. Tomorrow, the storm will clear, the sun will come out, and the beauty of the tide rolling into the cliffs will take my breath away. I know that there are dangers lurking in the darkest nights. But I have my compass and true North Star to direct me no matter where I go.

Navigating parenting is hard. Finding the strength to get through each day when one is carrying the hurt of loss or the burden of overwhelming circumstances often makes life feel unchartable. As friends, acquaintances, clients, and community members share their stories with me, I always find myself being reminded that my story is serving a purpose. The pain I have gone through with Isaac's birth story and subsequent special-needs journey have provided me with a guide map for others just starting to cross into this unknown territory. While no two journeys could possibly be the same, helping others to find their strength and offering them new resources to add to their toolbox gives me hope that, as a community, we can continue to teach each other new survival techniques.

My hope and my prayer for anyone struggling to understand the why of life's hardships is that it will forge connections with others. Ultimately, we are stronger together. With so many things that can divide us in today's society, I find comfort in seeing stories of support from unexpected places popping up in my social media feeds. There is no way that I will ever be able to repay the kindness of all the incredible people who have surrounded us on our journey thus far, so I pray that my testimony of Isaac finding his way home can pay it forward to someone else who needs to hear encouraging words in their moment of darkness.

Acknowledgments

I thank my God for you every time I think of you; and every time I pray for you all, I pray with joy.
—Philippians 1:3–4

To my husband, Andrew. Thank you for understanding and supporting my need, not only to document but also to share our family's journey. It has given me a space to continue to heal through encouraging and supporting others through our story.

To my son, Isaac. Thank you for making me a mama and for showing me what it looks like to love fiercely and trust God wholly. Thank you for sharing your joy and laughter with the world—we are better for it.

To my daughter, Siena. Thank you for giving me a chance to celebrate motherhood a second time with such grace, hope, and healing. You are the daughter I dreamed would complete our sweet family.

To my parents, Paul and Sylvia, your tireless support of my adventures in school, work, marriage, and parenthood has given me the opportunity to take risks and follow my heart. I am so thankful to watch you dive all in to your roles of Nana and Papa in this season of life. It is a privilege to raise our kids just down the street from you. They don't fully understand yet what a special thing it is to have their grandparents living in the same town. I think my continual finding my way back to Northern California speaks for itself just how much I value keeping family close. Thank you for grounding me when life threatens to sweep me away.

To my in-laws, Neil and Julie, thank you for all the ways you show up for our family with open arms. From long hours in the hospital with us, to watching the kids overnight so Andrew and I can recharge, and all the other little things you do—we are grateful our children can grow up spending time with you each week. Also, to my Hershey siblings, thanks Heidi (Bryan), Trevor, Austin, and C for being the best aunts and uncles our kids could ask for!

To my dear friend Cindy Linsenbardt. Thank you for the beautiful artwork you created for the cover of this book. God has been intertwining our lives for many years now, and I am so excited for continued opportunities to work together on projects in the future. Thank you also for connecting me with the wonderfully kind Cheryl Molin. Working with such a high-caliber editor on my debut book was a true honor.

To my talented friend and mentor, Bronwyn Lea. Thank you for so graciously offering your wisdom and professional insight during the process of this book. I sincerely value your opinion and am so grateful for the time you gave during your busy schedule to help me with all of the little details that make a big impact. Thank you also for introducing me to the lovely Charlotte Donlon. It was a huge blessing to have her thoughtful feedback on such a personal story.

To our Upward Church Norfolk friends. Thank you for stepping in as a familial community for us during our time stationed in Virginia. Specifically, to our friends Tommy and Laura Seigle, Marisa and Andy Muhs, Christy and Tim Johnson, and the beautiful couples in our first Bible study group.

To our birth team at Navy Medical Center Portsmouth. We are forever indebted to your expertise but, even more so, to your kindness and support. Specifically, I would like to thank Dr. Cobery, Dr. Piccirilli, Dr. Mayhew, and our developmental pediatric team.

Last but not least, to the Edmarc staff, volunteers, and supporting agencies. Debbie, Brittney, Madalyn, Kim, Kristin, and Shantel—I have never known people with such hearts of pure gold. Thank you for going above and beyond every single day. Your friendships changed me and my understanding of empathy and compassion. We are indebted to the Edmarc organization and the love and support y'all pour out on every person who walks through your doors.

Final shout-outs to friends from home who helped us in our transition back into the civilian world. My nanny family, the O'Malleys, Alyssa McGriff para/nanny/friend extraordinaire, and my ladies of FBC Davis 2x2. I love you and am so thankful for your friendship.

About the Author

Laura Hershberger is a master's level social worker, school counselor, military wife and, most recently, a special-needs mom. Her fifteen years of work with at-risk children in various capacities and their family's own journey with trauma fuels her dedication to providing educational resources and practical support to families facing life's challenges. Laura lives with her husband and two children in Northern California. *Isaac's Way Home: A Mother's Memoir* is her first book.

CPSIA information can be obtained
at www.ICGtesting.com
Printed in the USA
LVHW111151151120
671745LV00029B/336